Discerning Culture

II

Discerning Culture

Knowing the Depths of Scriptural Christianity in a Culture of Scriptural Indifference

Marlon De Blasio, Ph.D.

Canadian Evangel Publishing

To Christians everywhere who, like the child in the story of Hans Christian Andersen, are bravely discerning that, The Emperor has no clothes

Contents

Introduction

I thank you for considering *Discerning Culture*, with the hope of enriching your Christian faith. North American Christianity has been influenced by mainstream culture more than we care to admit. The language of Christian faith is becoming increasingly regressive to cultural ears. Yet Christianity remains very much alive. Many believers continue to desire the "abundant life" promised by Jesus, but our cultural context is making it difficult to experience. I have attempted to discern cultural thought, with the hope of providing a solution for the spiritual dilemma. Herein you will find what I believe are perspectives that will challenge you, make you think about Christian faith in culture, and will encourage you towards a deeper Scriptural experience. Perspectives are from a North American context, but there are parallel learnings for Christians in the Western world.

Of note, you will find that I have included Scriptural passages rather than citing only the references. This was intentional. Distractions are common nowadays, and I purposed to eliminate any that may hinder the reader from searching the Scriptures after noting the references. Also, I believe that seeing relevant Scriptures within the flow of reading provides a richer experience. Years ago, when I became a Christian, my first Bible was the KJV and I got comfortable with it, but eventually I transitioned to the NKJV and the ESV. For consistency, I have elected to use the NKJV (Thomas Nelson). Throughout the book I refer often to Scriptural Christianity and Christian faith, and I defined them in the initial footnotes and noted how they will be written as SC and CF.

If you are like me, you have probably wondered why anyone would place supplementary reading notes at the back? In my opinion, it's more convenient to see them on the same page below, rather than fumbling back and forth and interrupting the read. I am hoping that you will appreciate the footnote format as well.

I prayerfully wish you a worthwhile reading of *Discerning Culture*.

Acknowledgements

There are many who deserve gratitude for this production. My wife, Felicia, and our son, Nathan, provided ongoing support and input almost every other night at the dinner table. Nathan was instrumental in the fine tuning of the title. Felicia took the time to read the initial manuscript and alerted me to several points that required clarification and further development, which improved the book.

Discerning Culture was mostly written at the Horsey Library at Tyndale University College and Seminary. The Director of Library Services, Hugh Rendle, and his team, provided excellent service. I thank all the librarians and support staff for helping me with the research. I enjoyed immensely my time writing there.

I met many graduate students in the library and I took coffee breaks with some and chatted with others, and their conversations were theologically enriching and stimulating. One student in particular, Jesse James, who was writing a thesis, became my friend. We consumed plenty of coffee while we discussed Christian faith in culture, and the conversations were enjoyable. He may not agree with everything I have written, but I nevertheless owe him gratitude for having stimulated my thinking to write and produce some intriguing thoughts.

There are many professors, scholars, and Christian leaders with whom I chatted about my book, in person, by email, and on social media. They surely challenged me to produce something fresh. Dr. Harold Wells, Professor Emeritus, Emmanuel College, University of Toronto, was kind enough to spend quality time with me and provided much critical feedback. I gleaned several thoughts from our conversations that were both challenging and encouraging towards making my views clearer. He may not agree with all of my viewpoints, but he is a gracious scholar and I owe him many thanks.

The cover was designed by Bonnie Wong here in Toronto. Her artistry should be commended, and is highly appreciated.

Chapter 1

CHRISTIAN FAITH WITHIN A CULTURE OF SKEPTICISM

"Lord, I believe; help my unbelief" Mark 9:24

As a Christian, the depths of Scriptural Christianity[1] begin to be experienced when you realize that deep within you rests a conviction that it's true; moreover, that it's *real*. Perhaps this is ridiculously obvious to you or perhaps you think that it's not so critical because a believer grows along the way. There are those, however, within our faith communities whose Christian faith[2] has been suspended by unbelief. They could be a friend of yours, or the fellow believer sitting next to you at a small group, or maybe even your spouse. It's not that they have become unbelievers, but

---

[1] Scriptural Christianity will be written as SC. The Bible is trusted as authoritative for faith and practice, and SC seeks to know the Lord Jesus as revealed by the Spirit's inspired writers "to all generations" (Eph. 3:21), in order to enrich our relationship with Him and become effective disciples.

[2] Christian faith will be written as CF. Repentance and justification by faith alone, and by the acceptance of God's unmerited grace in the death and resurrection of Jesus, are what genuine CF is based upon. Regeneration provides the "New Birth" and the Spirit of God indwells a believer, with the onset of a personal and trusting relationship with Jesus. CF trusts Jesus as Lord and Saviour and allows a meaningful study of SC.

that they are inwardly crying, "Lord, I believe; help my unbelief." Some talk about it, but most keep it to themselves and continue to go through the motions. I remember years ago dropping off my son at primary school, and I would talk with another father in the parking area. He was a Christian too, and he knew of my theological interests and so he engaged me often in conversation about the nature of CF. He mentioned how he attended church with his wife and children, but his CF was suspended by unbelief. When talking with him, his struggles with CF were sadly evident on his countenance as he sought to express them. I have met many like him who nevertheless continue to participate in fellowship, and I even met students at theological schools where I studied who struggled with unbelief. They have all taught me a great deal, and I have developed a concern and appreciation for Christians who experience prolonged unbelief. Surely it is extremely challenging today for Christians to be serious about their beliefs in North American culture.

Culture is a broad term. Not everything about contemporary culture is inimical to SC. My particular criticism of our culture is how it is unfairly undermining CF. Thus, I attempt to show that the skepticism of secularism insinuated within culture requires discernment. Ironically, cultural thought is seeking to promote a manner of thinking towards values that it believes are good for society, and Christians are becoming conflicted. Trends are being established in culture which many believers are finding irresistible. Contemporary movies, music, television programs, documentaries, news outlets, commercials, art, literature, iconic personalities, brands, and even the expectations to succeed in a career, are all influencing a certain cultural identity. Culture seems to have a mysterious force that can trigger a particular mindset to influence our lives. In *Saving Leonardo*, Nancy Pearcey insightfully added that,

Today's most influential worldviews are born in the universities, but they touch all of us through the books we read, the music we listen to, and the movies we watch. Ideas penetrate our minds most deeply when communicated through the imaginative language of image, story, and symbol. It is crucial for Christians to learn how to 'read' that language and to identify worldview transmitted through cultural forms.[3]

Christians require discernment if they are to live the "abundant life" promised by Jesus (Jn. 10:10).

The discouragement of belief and the encouragement of skepticism towards CF are becoming a normal cultural trend. All believers are being affected by it. Even ardent believers are influenced by culture to simmer down their zeal and modify ministry to accommodate cultural sensitivities. As we get into the depths of SC, we also need to address the issues of doubt and unbelief, which are often caused not by legitimate criticism but by cultural dictation. Hopefully, we can learn something and encourage a brother or sister whose CF has been interrupted by unbelief.

If you are presently going through this phase you should know that there is hope to brighten your CF. I get it that bouts of unbelief can be frustrating for a Christian, especially after having "tasted the

---

[3] Nancy Pearcey, *Saving Leonardo: A Call to Resist the Secular Assault on Mind, Morals, & Meaning* (Nashville: B & H Publishing Group, 2010), 11.

good word of God and the powers of the age to come" (Heb. 6:5). Unbelief can cloud a believer's relationship with God, causing spiritual disorientation and the tenets of CF seem no longer believable. Unbelief can influence a Christian to seek answers among other religious and belief systems, because inward sentiments for God remain. Altogether, experiencing unbelief is never fun for a Christian. We cannot carry on as if doubt and unbelief are not present in our midst and thus are not issues of importance. Recently, a report from *Christianity Today* noted how struggles of doubt among young people in our churches are a concern that should not be kept silent:

> According to our study, which looked at 500 youth group graduates, over 70 percent of churchgoing high schoolers report having serious doubts about faith. Sadly, less than half of those young people shared their doubts and struggles with an adult or friend. . . In other words, it's not doubt that's toxic to faith; it's silence . . . But faith needs to be talked about and processed, and if these conversations diminish as our kids get older, we miss opportunities to help them remain fluent. [4]

Likewise another recent study noted "young people who had doubts . . . but were raised in an environment where they cannot talk about them with family or their church, thus allowing the

---

[4] Kara Powell, Steven Argue, "The Biggest Hindrance to Your Kids' Faith Isn't Doubt. It's Silence," *Christianity Today* (February 21, 2019), Online: *https://www.christianitytoday.com/ct/2019/february-web-only/doubt-parenting-biggest-hindrance-kids-faith-is-silence.html*

doubts to grow."[5] Not preparing ourselves will only make it worse, as doubt and unbelief continue to surface in our midst by cultural thought.

When they do surface the clichés are predictably heard: "pray more," "fast," "read the Bible," "read this author," and be sure to "listen to this sermon." Struggling believers have heard CF preached many times from the platform, on the radio, online, in meetings, with repeated utterances of "trust in the Lord," "walk in the Spirit," "believe God," and yet nothing life-changing ever occurred. We have been so quick to *tell* them what they should do. Fulfillment in the CF remains absent, and that is not how Christians should live for the Lord and be *told* to continue with clichés. If we continue by telling, we will not be doing any favours to those who are trying to overcome unbelief. As Christian leaders, we should seek to discern our cultural context, and learn how to explain SC so that believers can make real connections with God. As Blaise Pascal (1623-1662) said, "We are better persuaded by the reasons we discover ourselves than by those given to us by others."[6]

---

[5] Michael Gryboski, "Gen Z's 'lack of confidence' and 'confusion' over religious, moral issues presents major challenge," *Christian Post* (March 15, 2019), Online: *https://www.christianpost.com/news/gen-z-lack-of-confidence-confusion-religious-moral-issues.html*

[6] Martin H. Manser, comp. *The Westminster Collection of Christian Quotations* (Louisville: Westminster John Knox Press, 2001), 6.

Many whose CF is suspended are nevertheless seeking for the Lord Jesus beyond a weekly Sunday morning routine. Some do not reveal their unbelief or publicly ask hard questions for fear of being perceived less spiritual, or worse, face being shunned by Christian friends. Meanwhile a genuine yearning persists within a Christian during occasions of unbelief to regain the "peace of God, which surpasses all understanding" (Philip. 4:7). Let us note well that God does not abandon a believer during times of unbelief. For it is certain that, "If we are faithless, He remains faithful, He cannot deny Himself" (2 Tim. 2:13).

Now a state of unbelief in CF differs from having doubts about it. The former experience *suspends* CF from believing and trusting in its promises, fulfillments, and feels disconnected from God. It simply ceases from relating to Jesus as revealed by CF and from experiencing His relevancy in their daily lives. In short, CF has lapsed into an ineffectual spiritual state that no longer experiences God's peace. As the Israelites, for instance, who desired the rest of God but "could not enter in because of unbelief" (Heb. 3:19). Doubt differs, because it usually questions an aspect of CF or the nature of SC or a portion of Scripture, and certainly it can even question or doubt a particular biblical event, or an attribute of God. Doubt also causes a believer to consider seriously whether a particular doctrine of SC can apply today. Doubt does not necessarily *suspend* CF or cease from believing in its essential doctrines. Questioning and critically thinking about CF are not necessarily bad, because they can provide learnings that enrich the understanding and shape believers into deeper thinkers. As an author attests in *Cultural Intelligence*:

Few things have tempted me to abort my participation in the journey toward cultural intelligence as much as the tiring, painful process of questioning the assumptions on which my faith is based. But persevering through the disorienting course has led me to an intensified passion and pursuit of Jesus. The times of wrestling with your faith and doctrine are part of what moves you along the pathway to better loving God . . . Our doubts, questions, and probes into the mysterious waters beneath the tip of the iceberg are often what God uses most to change us so that we can be part of changing the world.[7]

All Christians experience doubt at one time or another and many emerge with a stronger CF and deeper experience of SC. I am addressing the believer's suspension of CF by *unbelief*, and in today's culture no believer is immune.

Or maybe your CF has become *stale*. This is even more common today. Staleness of CF causes a spiritual overcast and so the bright rays of the Spirit cease from shining in your life. Belief remains present, but it lacks that freshness with God and CF is not affecting one's life as it once did. In any case, when left to germinate, staleness of CF can also suspend believers from enjoying SC and from becoming happy participators in a fellowship. Attendance at church takes on more of a social or routine exercise, with little interest in faith talk. There exists a great

---

[7] David A. Livermore, Chap Clark (series ed.), *Cultural Intelligence: Improving Your CQ to Engage Our Multicultural World* (Grand Rapids: Baker Academic, 2009), 190.

opportunity for Christian leaders to invigorate our clichés, and apply biblical substance to the matter.

Sadly, cultural influence often leads believers to surrendering their CF and to de-convert in order to end the struggle of wrestling spiritually and intellectually. Some say that their de-conversion freed them from the experience of conflicting CF. It began with a doubt here, a doubt there, and then another which all went unsatisfied by the clichés, until the towel of unbelief was thrown into the rink of turmoil. Additionally, the intimidating forces of cultural icons overwhelmed their struggle and the pressure was insurmountable, resulting in a complete abandonment of CF. What I am encouraging for anyone going through a troubling period of unbelief is to hold on to your inner cry of "Lord I believe; help my unbelief," because if you have been born of God it's unmistakably there. Deal with your doubts one by one, and be reasonable with the expectations. I also hope that you do not blame yourself. You have been uniquely gifted by God. You can analyze your doubts one by one, and with His help and those of us who care you can deepen your knowledge and experience of CF.

All regenerated believers have a desire to love the Lord "with all your heart, with all your soul, with all your mind, and with all your strength" (Mk. 12:30). As difficult as it is, you really wish you could also "love your neighbour as yourself" (Mk. 12:31). I note the following tearfully. Hypocrisy is often found in our faith communities. Betrayal among believing friends is also not uncommon. As the Psalmist also experienced, "Even my own familiar friend in whom I trusted, Who ate my bread, Has lifted up his heel against me" (Ps. 42:9). So is unkindness towards one another, as well as jealousies, envies, covetousness, selfishness, and even narcissism, but we should seek and pursue "the knowledge of the Son of God, to a perfect man, to the measure of the stature of the fullness of Christ" (Eph. 4:13). When going through a phase of unbelief one should not allow the behavioural shortcomings of other Christians to dampen one's own search for fulfillment in CF. After all, we don't worship human beings; we worship Jesus. If our CF were dependent on the behaviour of Christians then we would all be in a state of unbelief, but it's not.

First and foremost, you must cultivate an understanding that, "without faith it is impossible to please Him, for he who comes to God must believe that He is, and that He is a rewarder of those who diligently seek Him" (Heb. 11:6). Faith alone is what will affirm the biblical promises in a believer's life. One's cognitive endeavour at studying and interpreting CF in hope of spiritual advancement can never suffice on its own. It can enrich one's thinking of CF but it can never establish a substitute "for the faith which was once . . . delivered to the saints" (Jude:3). You should realize that you have a direct inner working of grace with the undeniable witness of the Holy Spirit. Afterwards, your study of Scripture, of theology, of Christian and non-Christian literature, and your discernment of culture, will enrich your relationship with Jesus and your God given gifts and talents will flourish. Everyone you engage with will notice the difference.

Within every Christian the Spirit wants to accomplish a real sense of *knowingness*. God said, "Be still, *and know*, that I am God" (Ps. 46:10). Belief and knowingness are also separate matters. The man in Mark 9:24 believed, but lacked *knowingness,* which only the Lord Jesus could have provided. The man's plea wished for a certain outcome which he knew could happen, but his unbelief in

17

the matter *suspended* the desired outcome, as he lacked *knowingness*. Listen to what the Apostle Paul testified, *"I know whom I have believed and am persuaded that He is able to keep what I have committed to Him until that Day"* (2 Tim. 1:12). Paul's experience of *knowingness* superseded belief, and his "persuasion" strengthened his ultimate expectation of "that day." Paul sought to teach a deeper spiritual understanding of CF by a sense of knowingness: "The eyes of your understanding being enlightened that *you may know* what is . . . the exceeding greatness of His power towards us who believe" (Eph. 1:18-19). You have committed to CF and so why settle ensconced for years when you can press towards knowingness? If Christ has truly entered your life, what could possibly be greater than to know "the unsearchable riches of Christ" (Eph. 3:8). Note how J. I. Packer valued the pursuit of CF in his epochal making book, *Knowing God*:

> What makes life worthwhile is having a big enough objective, something which catches our imagination and lays hold of our allegiance; and this the Christian has, in a way that no other man has. For what higher, more exalted, and more compelling goal can there be than to know God?[8]

Perhaps some may point out that Packer wrote that in the '70s, and now our CF resides in a far different culture. This notation is not without merit, but SC requires of us to serve the Master who "is the same yesterday and today and forever" (Heb. 13:8).

---

[8] J. I. Packer, *Knowing God* (Downers Grove, ILL: InterVarsity Press, 1977), 30.

Yet secularism is giving us a "run for our money" unlike any previous epoch. As one Pastor keenly observed:

Concurrent with the cultural decline of the Christian narrative, numerous other valid interpretive schemes have presented themselves. Many of them connect more directly to the lived experience of our congregants simply because they are promoted by the multiple channels our people regularly draw from: pop culture, news, the Internet, and more. Hence, while the mainline Christian story may appear alive and well within the walls of the congregation, outside the church all these other valid sources from which to construct a religious identity are giving traditional Christian faith a run for its money.[9]

In culture, our precious CF is increasingly being perceived as an activity relegated to a Sunday morning tradition. We need to *know* what SC means in our lives. This lofty objective of knowing Christ is not received by an instant zap of the Spirit, which makes you spiritually indomitable and able to discern culture immediately with amazing acumen. It is, rather, an "anointing" that God bestows *especially* upon *you* as a believer so that knowingness is gradually taught to you by a direct growing experience with Jesus: "But the anointing which you have received from Him abides in you, and . . . teaches you concerning all things, and is true, and is not a lie" (1 Jn. 2:27).

---

[9] David J. Lose, *Preaching at the Crossroads: How the World - and our Preaching - is Changing* (Minneapolis, MN: Fortress Press, 2013), 102.

The quest for knowingness thus requires an intentional focus on what the grace of God has begun in your life. You became the person Jesus was referring to in His parabolic teaching of the merchant seeking a beautiful pearl. Jesus taught, "the kingdom of heaven is like a merchant seeking beautiful pearls, who when he had found one pearl of great price, went and sold all that he had and bought it" (Matt. 13:45-46). Your discovery of the beautiful pearl, who is Jesus, revealed a taste of heaven in your soul, with an enriched understanding of values which warranted Him as the central spot in your life ("went and sold all that he had and bought it"). You probably still have no issues with Jesus as your personal King, but culture around you is fiercely challenging.

Note well, I mean really well: our CF and values will never be acknowledged by cultural thought as a "beautiful pearl." "As Christians," wrote William A. Dembski, "we must not confuse making our faith credible to the world with seeking its approval. Craving the world's approval is a sure way to perdition." [10] Questions about CF should be studied and legitimately asked, but one's CF is not based on whether it can satisfy criteria established by culture as to what should and shouldn't qualify for belief in SC. So do not agonize when your faith is not persuasive to others as it is to you. Do not agonize when it is delicious to you and distasteful in culture. Do not agonize over why the Gospel makes sense to you but dismissed as nonsense by cultural thought. Moreover, do

---

[10] William A. Dembski, *The End of Christianity: Finding a Good God in an Evil World* (Nashville: B & H Publishing Group, 2009), 5.

not agonize over why the values of SC are precious to you, but culture ridicules them incessantly.

Note also how you experience the veracity of this Scripture as you interact with cultural thought: "For the message of the cross is foolishness to those who are perishing, but to us who are being saved it is the power of God" (1 Cor. 1:18). The Apostle Paul continued,

> Now we have received, not the spirit of the world, but the Spirit who is from God, that we might know the things that have been freely given to us by God . . . But the natural man does not receive the things of the Spirit of God, for they are foolishness to him; nor can he know them, because they are spiritually discerned (1 Cor. 2:12, 14).

Remember, Jesus said authoritatively: "Most assuredly I say to you unless one is born again, he cannot see the kingdom of God. . . . You must be born again" (Jn. 3:3-7). Regeneration introduced you to a new spiritual reality even as you continued to interact within your society. Culture is being shaped by "the natural man" (more on this later) who "does not receive the things of the Spirit of God." The communication of your CF to an unregenerate mind is usually received with resistance, or dismissed kindly as maybe good for you but not necessarily for everyone. Thus, the frustrations you experience when you interact within a culture that cannot appreciate your regenerate state of mind.

Of course, the Christian mind has much in common with the unregenerate mind. They can share in a mutual understanding of business, laws, democratic processes, civility, even natural theology, and a lot more, but not in an understanding of God's special revelation in Jesus Christ. You who have been born-again can appreciate that CF is a divine work of God, but the natural mind will perceive it today as no better than a person's particular choice of religious belief. That is also why many Christian students become extremely frustrated with their professors who are committed to secularism and dismissive of a believer's direct experience of CF. Be encouraged, however, by what Paul said, "The Spirit Himself bears witness with our spirit that we are children of God" (Rom. 8:16). The personal experience of God's grace cannot be discounted, for it can be unmistakable.

The frustration is especially acute when scathing criticisms come from people whom cultural thought considers smart, intellectual, sophisticated, successful, and from those holding prestigious positions in universities. The culture's mentality is that if a scientist says something, it ought to receive official credence. Who are you to disagree? Can you possibly know better than a decorated professor at a distinguished university? More than a scientist on the Discovery channel? The usurpation of thought by a prestigious position can easily intimidate a Christian, and consequently clouds of unbelief suspend connections with God. It is so apropos here what we read in Proverbs: "The fear of man brings a snare" (29:25). Many believers are losing confidence in their CF because of what they are believing about the source of the criticism, whereas a proper evaluation should consider only the merits of what is presented regardless of who is the presenter.

Should you master only one thing from reading this book I would that you fear not cultural thought's punditry of skepticism towards CF, and not accept its validity because a cultural icon says so. You must discern the merits of what is proposed, while not being confused by the position or reputation of the communicator.

Honestly ask yourself how much undermining of CF has influenced you because of much consideration for the source's prestigious position? How often have you allowed your inward convictions of SC, which you knew deep down were true, to be forfeited or negotiated because of culture pressure? Had you concentrated strictly on the content regardless of the presenter, wouldn't you have thought differently?

To illustrate, consider this: you walk into a shoemaker's shop and you over hear the shoemaker comment about the universe. Saying, "I believe that as we observe the universe and learn of its laws our understanding leads us to conclude that the universe came from other previous laws, and consequently we now have a fully functioning universe able to guide people in all areas of society." You would probably smile while thinking how illogical and non-sensical it all sounds, and even wonder how anybody could believe that. You would definitely not leave the shop with a crisis of faith. You would probably smile at the shoemaker and leave with your bag saying, "Thank you and have a nice day."

What if those exact comments did not come from a local shoemaker, but you heard them on a television documentary featuring a scientist from a big-name university? When you heard the shoemaker, you left thinking that it sounded absurd. After the documentary featuring exactly what the shoemaker said you're probably thinking, "Lord, help my unbelief." Again, the supposed prestigious *source* of the presentation is what often causes spiritual consternation for a believer in today's culture, and not the content itself. "What this all goes to show," assessed John C. Lennox, "is that nonsense remains nonsense, even when talked by world-famous scientists."[11]

Unfortunately, the negative undertones to CF by famous scientists are sometimes *dogmatized* blindly by culture with effective intimidation on believers. When it comes to science it should be respected and appreciated. Society has benefitted greatly from the contributions of scientific enterprise, and we should encourage its advancement. Christians who are qualified to do science have also made, and continue to make, great contributions. We should acknowledge, however, that cultural thought is being influenced by "scientism," and that is different from science. Basically, scientism is an ideology that promotes a scientific activity beyond the realms of science. Such an approach is not yet an established cultural trend, but scientism sure is beginning to influence cultural thought. It highlights legitimate science and mixes in an ingredient of Humanism in an attempt to answer the questions of life free from God.

Of course, if a meteorologist, whether Christian or not, reports that a hurricane is coming then we should prepare, but meteorology cannot prescribe scientifically on whether it is morally right or wrong to loot from abandoned properties. Science has made life easier, but it cannot provide all of the answers to our deepest questions, because it is not equipped to deal with them.

---

[11] John C. Lennox, *God and Stephen Hawking: Whose Design is it Anyway?* (Oxford, EN: Lion Hudson, 2011), 32. Lennox earned a Ph.D. in mathematics, and a Ph.D. in philosophy and has revealed plenty of inconsistencies presented to the public by famous scientists.

Yet there are some highly influential figures who are seeking to apply a manufactured version of scientific thought even to moral values, to our emotional needs, and to questions about God. It is notable how their methodologies take the liberty to frame theological beliefs in a manner that disqualify a believer from doing *proper* science. In *The Moral Landscape: How Science Can Determine Human Values*, for example, Sam Harris wrote:

There is an epidemic of scientific ignorance in the United States. This isn't surprising, as very few scientific truths are self-evident and many are deeply counterintuitive. It is by no means obvious that empty space has structure or that we share a common ancestor with both the housefly and the banana. It can be difficult to think like a scientist (even, we have begun to see, when one is a scientist). But it would seem that few things make thinking like a scientist more difficult than an attachment to religion.[12]

---

[12] Sam Harris, *The Moral Landscape: How Science Can Determine Human Values* (New York: Free Press, 2010), 176. I enjoyed reading this book, and found it interesting. What undermines the intellectual integrity of the book is how he frames belief in God by selected personal views that are assumed as non-negotiable. To be fair, the citation is preceded by Harris's critique of some of Francis Collins's work as a scientist, as well as his Christian beliefs. I would agree with Harris that some of Collins's work appeared weak. My point is that Harris could have critiqued the scientific work by its own merits, without a religious conversation. Then again, criticism of CF stirs emotions, and probably adds to the book's provocation.

The last sentence is a sweeping opinion, and not a scientific conclusion. What about a scientist who is attached to art? Music? Personal meditation? Why should anyone care? Shouldn't scientific work be evaluated by its own merits? Shouldn't we separate scientific work from the personal lifestyle of a scientist? I think Harris would want us to consider his work by its own merits. By commenting that, "an attachment to religion" somehow prevents "thinking like a scientist," reveals his personal dislike. Proponents of scientism seem motivated by their own likes, opinions, and aversions, especially ones about God. In cultural thought, such sentiments are increasingly being promoted as on par with pure science.

All human beings are morally depraved before our Maker and possess a natural dislike for Him. We must acknowledge that even cultural icons have frailties, shortcomings, biases, and in their depravity a general aversion for CF. May sound trite, but the Christian mind could benefit by seriously acknowledging that human beings, regardless of education, celebrity status, or distinguished accomplishments, should not be deified. I once heard a Caribbean preacher say, "Everyone puts on their pants one leg at a time." Scientists, educators, pundits, and celebrities are very human and susceptible to the foregoing like everyone else. No cultural icon is "larger than life." Yet the hoopla surrounding what a celebrity says is now often leveraged exponentially by cultural thought. So, if you accept something based on one's authority or their apparent popular status in culture, think again.

We are now grappling with a skepticism in cultural thinking towards CF by the punditry of popular figures that is becoming obstinate. Even sound and cogent corrections from highly

26

qualified Christian intellectuals are not easily overcoming the contemporary cultural consciousness of secular thinking. For example, in 2009, Dinesh D'Souza debated Christopher Hitchens on the question, "What's So Great About God?" In his opening statements Hitchens made the usual points of secular humanism with no rational interconnectedness (i.e., humanity is fine on its own and knowledge is increasing for the betterment of humankind and religion continues to stifle). D'Souza keenly discerned the incoherencies in Hitchens's reasoning and began by saying,

> When I first came to America from India as an exchange student I was assigned to live in Arizona. One of my first entertainments was to go to a Rodeo. I feel like I am back at the Rodeo. By which I mean in listening to Christopher Hitchens I see a point here, a point there, *but also a lot of bull in between.*[13]

Of course, this was comical, even Hitchens was amused, but D'Souza made an effective point. As a sharp thinker, he had immediately discerned the non-sensical reasoning of Hitchens and went on to present a rational belief in God. In my opinion, however, debates often take on a peculiarity where arguments do not seem to matter as much as popular appeal. Hitchens's skepticism was charismatically influential, even though much of what he said was "smoke and mirrors."

---

[13] "What's So Great About God?" Christopher Hitchens (1949-2011) and Dinesh D'Souza, Online, *https://www.youtube.com/watch?v=ss5r0xsPVU0*, at 44:15.

The overall antipathy of culture towards God cannot be denied, and the skepticism can be seductive. Note this quotation from a contemporary and highly regarded philosopher, which was uttered about twenty years ago but I believe has come to characterize contemporary cultural thought:

> I want atheism to be true and am made uneasy by the fact that some of the most intelligent and well informed people I know are religious believers. It isn't just that I don't believe in God and, naturally, hope that I am right in my belief. It's that I hope there is no God! I don't want there to be a God; I don't want the universe to be like that.[14]

Cultural thought does not "want there to be a God." Aversion now wraps itself with an aura of philosophical sophistication that is gradually being accepted by culture as the bright side, and the faith side as dull. Cultural thought is beginning to discourage the cogency of any inference to God, and prefers the "bright" side of skepticism. Effective CF should nevertheless understand itself as anchored to the revealed truths of SC, which have *withstood the test of time*. Centuries of attack on the validity of CF have not eliminated the grace of God from impacting lives today more than ever.

On the other hand, skepticism encourages everyone to be open minded and ask hard questions, but skeptics rarely apply the same rigour to their own beliefs. Intellectual Christians in various

---

[14] Thomas Nagel, *The Last Word* (Oxford: Oxford University Press, 1997), 130-31. The quote is not intended to cast any aspersions on the philosophical competency of Nagel. Rather, it is used here to highlight the honest inner feelings of some well-respected professors towards God which can influence culture.

disciplines have risen up to provide brilliant cumulative presentations that warrant the reasonableness of CF and how its classical language remains relevant. They have made remarkable progress in keeping the beliefs of SC in the conversation of many disciplines. Conversations with those who hold a counter perspective are held all the time, but cultural thought continues with an attitude of "so what?" Influencers of culture listen casually and then lapse with persistence on the same old questions which detract from further inferential reflection, such as, "Okay, who made God" (This question will be addressed in Chapter 4)?

Some Christians are tempted to believe that perhaps there aren't any good reasons for faith; it's simply something you choose to believe. Others become exasperated and ask themselves, why doesn't God please come out of hiding and reveal Himself? I truly empathize towards such a believer's frustration, even though the latter request does not grasp what is being requested of God. First of all, what is the actual expectation? Even if you had a "burning bush" experience it would still not satisfy you - later you would question whether that experience was real or not and then ask for another, and so on. What the plea is earnestly asking for is a personal inner sense of *knowingness* that will provide substance for faith, and that has been revealed by God.

By now, some of you are probably thinking that I am being overly critical of North American culture. After all, not everything about it is so detrimental to CF. I do realize that behind cultural thought there are people, and that not all have intentions to malign CF. Culture's skepticism, however, has ratcheted up its criticism to shrilling noises and it is necessary to emphasize meticulous discernment. Nonetheless cultural thought is influencing some believers to accept CF as partly okay and partly not okay for today. The temptation now is to accept the criticism of cultural thought as the "cool" version, because that is how it is being framed. Consequently, this sort of unbelief begins to perceive CF as largely outdated and mostly irrelevant. Sadly, the mocking of God is disturbing and offending less. Jesus also begins to be perceived as definitely not the only way to God. We were forewarned a long time ago by Paul about the presence of these contemporary "seducing spirits" (1 Tim. 4:1).

Amidst the struggle, God can seem a galactic distance away, but know assuredly that He is actually breathtakingly near. How can God be near when unbelief is suspending the fulfillment of CF? Well, it's not God who moved away from you. Remember that when God created humankind, He "breathed into his nostrils the breath of life; and man became a living being" (Gen. 2:7). The very breath you are now inhaling and exhaling to become "a living being" was given to you by God. That is how near He is to you. Be open-minded to Him, enlarge your inner most being, and genuinely consider another of His promises: "And you will seek Me and find Me, when you search for Me with all your heart" (Jer. 29:13).

As a Christian's unbelief searches for answers, the quest should try not to assess God through the same grid with which it assesses the natural world. In other words, it should not tempt God with unreasonableness by seeking to place Him under a microscope and expecting data to emerge. Such an expectation will never be realized, because it is categorically misguided. The revelations of SC do not claim to provide a scientific treatise on how the workings of God can be directly observed, tested, and calculated.

Natural revelation has its place, but God Himself is not personally known empirically. It is unreasonable to expect to see and descriptively assess Him in order to justify CF. A believer must distinguish the external experience of material things from the internal experience of God's Kingdom. This dynamic must be acknowledged, "while we do not look at the things which are seen, but at the things which are not seen. For the things which are seen are temporary, but the things which are not seen are eternal" (2 Cor. 4:18).

The impossibility of proving God by empirical attestation is exactly where culture is gradually being influenced to go. Skepticism is claiming that God's existence cannot be proven by the scientific method, and therefore faith is a blind choice made for emotional comforts. Most people are not aware of the scientific method's scope, particularly that a hypothesis is proposed, examined for predictability and repeatability, falsifiable outcomes considered, and then results concretely explained. Yet cultural thought isn't noting how the scientific method is not purposed to prove or disprove what it cannot experience empirically. When we listen to an enthralling piece of music can the scientific method falsify whether it was riveting or not? When we experience beauty in something can the scientific method falsify our appreciation? When sports announcers say that a team played with "heart" can the scientific method prove otherwise? As Pascal famously said, "The heart has its reasons, which reason knows not, as we feel in a thousand instances."[15]

---

[15] Manser, *The Westminster Collection of Christian Quotations*, 164.

What remains fascinating is that the question of God does not seem to be fading away, but continues to rage in culture. A few years ago, I attended a debate here in Toronto on the question, Has Science Made God Irrelevant? The venue was packed to capacity. Afterwards, I approached the presenter who defended the affirmative answer. After some friendly bantering I mentioned how he presented a spaghetti monster in the form of a small puppet in order to emphasize some of his points. That is, one cannot prove the existence of God as one cannot prove if there is a spaghetti monster and so belief in either one is essentially imaginary. Then I asked him, "If the question of the debate had been changed to, Has Science Made the Spaghetti Monster Irrelevant? Would we have had a packed house?" We both knew there would have been an audience of zero. So, he smiled spontaneously, and politely asked me, "What is your point?"

"My point," I explained, "is that when you put God into the question people show up because God is *compelling.*"

He paused and replied, "I'll give you that."

Within our human constitution there is definitely something which continues to find God compelling. He convicts us of His existence in very real ways. His Spirit seems to do something to both believers and unbelievers. Jesus did say that when the Spirit "has come, he will convict the world of sin, and of righteousness, and of judgement" (Jn 16:8). This is precisely what has happened. Humankind, whether it admits it or not, finds God irresistible and this conviction will always be haunting. This is why unbelief can cause a lifelong preoccupation with God for some former believers.

Note the story of Michael Shermer, the editor in chief of the magazine, *Skeptic*,[16] who has been described as an agonistic, non-theist, atheist, but likes to identify as a skeptic. In the 1970s, as a senior high schooler, he became a Christian. In 2009 he wrote:

> I have spent my entire adult life thinking about God - 30 plus years cogitating on a being that may or may not even exist. Although I am no longer a believer, I still think about him more than I care to admit. Once I stopped believing in God in the late 1970s, I thought that the whole issue of God's existence or non-existence would simply fall by the way-side as I devoted more and more of my personal life to family, friends, travel, and avocations. And yet for a concatenation of reasons involving both my personal and professional lives, God just won't go away.[17]

Of course, "God just won't go away." Why would He? He is the ultimate truth which continually impresses on our hearts and minds. "He is there," Francis Schaeffer (1912-1984) once noted in

---

[16] The magazine is not strictly focused on the question of God's existence. It covers topics about urban myths, superstitions, mass hysterias, faith healers, fad diets, and what it deems as pseudo-science.

[17] Michael Shermer, "How to Think About God: Theism, Atheism, and Science," In *50 Voices of Disbelief: Why We Are Atheists*, Russell Blackford and Udo Schuklenk, eds. (New York: Wiley-Blackwell, 2009), 65.

a book, "and He is not silent."[18] Shermer explained how his university courses and professors steered him towards unbelief. His journey from belief to skepticism is not uncommon. My encouragement to anyone who is struggling with decades old unbelief is to stop and begin to think boldly for yourself, and do not allow the pressure of cultural biases to influence you. Make up your own mind. Think upon where your unbelief originated. What good reasons led you to yield and cleave to unbelief?

The origins were most likely from a source of prestige or authority. You may say that it came from contemporary scientific thought. Please keep thinking, because it did not come from science but from a *human interpretation of science* and promoted favourably by cultural forces. You may even think that it came from a professional peer reviewed process. It certainly did not. The peer review process is a gate keeping stewardship of professionals who only allow publications by those who think like them. Rarely will anything that seems to substantiate faith in God pass by them. Even so, no human generated process can claim an ultimate authority over how humankind should learn. The Lord Jesus is the only One who can claim sovereignty over humankind, because He was more than a man. That is why He alone is "the way, the truth, and the life" (Jn. 14:6); "And you shall know the truth, and the truth shall make you free" (Jn. 8:32). Seriously mark this Scripture as a personal rule: "For what if some did not believe? Will their

---

[18] Francis Schaeffer, *He is there and He is not silent* (Wheaton, Ill: Tyndale House Publishers, 1972).

unbelief make the faithfulness of God without effect? Certainly not! Indeed, let God be true but every man a liar" (Rom. 3: 3-4). Shermer's unbelief began in university as he interacted with his professors and peers. Now I am by no means discouraging a Christian from attending university. I have attended universities in Canada and the USA. A university education today is indispensable, but make no mistake about the secular humanist indoctrination at universities in Western countries. I use the word "indoctrination" because secular humanism instructs with an intentionality that discourages any dissent, disloyalty, or criticism, and questioning it is always demurred. Anyone who rises up in a university and seriously criticizes it in favour of CF will surely be considered aberrant, and possibly become the object of scorn. In *The Abolition of Man*, C. S. Lewis (1898-1963) analyzed how educators can influence a particular manner of thinking in students. He wrote allegorically (and prophetically) about an actual high school text book:

> For the power of Man to make himself what he pleases means, as we have seen, the power of some men to make other men what *they* please. In all ages, no doubt, nurture and instruction have, in some sense, attempted to exercise this power. . . . But the man moulders of the new age will be armed with the powers of an omnicompetent state and an irresistible scientific technique: we shall get at last a race of conditioners who really can cut out all posterity in what shape they please.[19]

---

[19] C. S. Lewis, *The Abolition of Man* (Glasgow: Williams Collins Sons & Co. Ltd., sixth impression, 1986), 37.

Today, the "omnicompetence" of secular thought pervades education and is influencing culture with "irresistible" forces that seriously challenge CF. Somehow culture has adopted the view that, in pretty much all matters, secular thought is more objective. In other words, Christian thought is perceived as characterized with biases while the proponents of secularism are perceived objectively more reliable. This is one of the reasons for the rise in skepticism. Cultural thought, however, should learn a lesson from history and realize that skepticism has itself been ridden with bias, which continues to this day.

One of the founding fathers of contemporary skepticism towards CF was Bertrand Russell (1872-1970). When we search beyond the accolades attributed to him, we learn about a thinker tainted with strict and unfair biases towards CF. He refused to consider any of it. In 1975, Lady Katharine Tait (1923-), the biological daughter of Russell and his second wife Dora Black (1894-1986), wrote an intriguing book, *My Father Bertrand Russell*. Tait recounted her relationship with him and what it was like growing up in the Russell household. Her parents established Beacon Hill School in their home so that their children, and others, "could be educated as they thought proper."[20] Apparently, there existed no encouragement to think freely and pursue the evidence wherever it led. As Tait wrote,

> My father . . . always wanted us to consider both sides and then make up our minds. 'Considering both sides' meant hearing the

---

[20] Katharine Tait, *My Father Bertrand Russell* (New York: HBJ Publishing, 1975), 69.

opinions on both sides as well as studying the facts. . . . The bias of the teacher was always allowed to show, provided he or she took the trouble to present the other side also. In practice, at Beacon Hill, 'making up our own minds' usually meant agreeing with my father, . . . we heard 'the other side' only from people who disagreed with it. There was never a cogent presentation of the Christian faith, for instance, from someone who really believed it.[21]

Why didn't Russell allow a presentation on CF from a qualified proponent? If CF is untrue and intellectually untenable what is the fear? Christian schools sometime invite atheists to present their counter-perspective to CF. Christian students also read primary atheistic literature. Like Russell's school, however, most skeptics are often not open to educating themselves from primary teachers on the merits of CF, choosing to learn about it from those who are already skeptical.

Tait eventually became a Christian, attended seminary, and served as a missionary with her husband. "For me," she testified, "the belief in forgiveness and grace was like sunshine after long days of rain. No matter what I did, . . . God would be there to forgive."[22] She wished this experience for her father:

I would have liked to convince my father that I had found what he had been looking for, the ineffable something he had longed for all his life. I would have liked to persuade him that the

---

²¹ Ibid., 94.

²² Ibid., 188.

search for God does not have to be vain. But it was hopeless. He had known too many blind Christians, bleak moralists who sucked the joy from life and persecuted their opponents; he would never have been able to see the truth they were hiding.[23]

As Tait mentions, her father searched for inward peace throughout his life. Russel wrote a poem which revealed his unsettled life in atheism:

Through the long years,
I have sought peace,
I found ecstasy,
I found anguish,
I found madness,
I found loneliness,
I found the solitary pain
that gnaws the heart,
But peace I did not find.[24]

Tait's life, however, has shown that unbelief can be conquered to discover the depths and beauty of God's grace in Jesus. Tait even tried to share her joyous CF with her unbelieving father. She was not intimidated by his iconic stature in the culture of the time. Her experience of God's love and grace was too strong for that.

Now the most frustrating question of all for CF, surely remains: If God is so loving and kind why does He allow pain and suffering in the world? Almost everyone acknowledges that some

---

[23] Ibid., 189.

[24] Ray Monk, *Bertrand Russell-The Spirit of Solitude 1872-1921* (New York: Free Press, 1996), xix.

of it is caused by human actions. Human beings are the cause of wars, violence, pollution resulting in disease, exploitation of the poor, and fatal accidents. Our human experience is marked by free-will. Even our judicial system presupposes free-will, and functions to adjudicate the accountable actions of law breakers. People have transgressed laws and perpetrated much evil on themselves. Yet God desires happiness for everyone. Happiness was a primary teaching of Jesus: "These things I have spoken to you, that my joy may remain in you and that your joy may be full" (Jn. 15:11). Regardless, the question will return: Why does God allow these evils among humankind? When an earthquake, tornado or tsunami cause devastation then the question really frustrates CF. It would seem prima facie that unbelief in God legitimizes itself in times of natural calamities.

Personally, my heart always goes out to those who experience pain and suffering, and I wish I had the power to do more. I have also come to realize that philosophical and theological explanations do not alleviate human pain and suffering. Countless treatises have been written by deep thinkers throughout the centuries on the problem of evil. It still remains the kingpin of issues in conversations about God's existence. I think that the reason why we immediately invoke God during an experience of pain and suffering is because He is the only One who can really help. Philosophers and theologians may inform the intellect on the issue of God and evil, but they can never satisfy or comfort a mother whose child is suffering. A contemporary Christian philosopher describes a personal incident, and it is silencing:

> Some of my reflections about suffering began with a conversation I had with my aunt Regina many years ago at a

family gathering. . . . She spoke with me about how difficult it was for her son Charles . . . suffer from a serious mental illness . . . I began to tell Aunt Regina some of my more abstract, philosophical explanations for why God might allow evils such as Charles's suffering. But after listening very graciously, Aunt Regina turned to me and said, 'But Vince, that doesn't speak to me as a mother.'[25]

Pain and suffering calls for comfort deep within by everyone, with the hope of possibly overcoming a personal calamity. Unpacking the problem of evil intellectually, though required, cannot satisfy the emotional hurts of people.

The problem of evil takes real significance on an emotional level. So, if God does not exist then what comfort can Humanism provide? In an atheistic worldview evil is ultimately the product of material forces gone awry. On what basis can Humanism rule that evil is bad if there is no ultimate moral law to recognize good? Whenever evil occurs in the world atheists also moralize as they consider that it ought not to be so. Humanity's innate capacity for consolation is inescapable. It's as Paul M. Gould comments in *Cultural Apologetics*,

Our innate longings lead us, if we pay attention to them, to desire a better world, a world that has faded from conscious memory, yet that memory persists in our hearts. Deep within

---

[25] Ravi Zacharias, Vince Vitale, *Why Suffering: Finding Meaning and Comfort When Life Doesn't Make Sense* (New York: Faith Words, 2014), 59.

the human conscience, we find an unexplainable longing for wholeness, justice, and a meaningful life. We long to experience life 'the way it was meant to be,' even if we cannot explain why we think it should be that way . . . [26]

Now imagine reiterating Richard Dawkins's explanation to a suffering person: "The universe we observe has ... no design, no purpose, no evil and no good, nothing but blind, pitiless indifference. ... DNA neither knows nor cares. . . . And we dance to its music."[27] No suffering people would accept this explanation as the truth, and even if they did there is no hope of consolation, for our "DNA neither knows nor cares." It is as if to say, too bad and so sad but that's the way it is and so the only real choice is to put up with it. The fact that we experience this view as emotionally cold and unconscionable demonstrates that our DNA does care. The foregoing comments of Dawkins are also a great example of how to differentiate content from presenter. So again, it is vital to train ourselves to perceive that, "nonsense remains nonsense, even when talked by world-famous scientists."

Even if Humanism were true, what hope could it offer to comfort the emotional pain caused by the blind, purposeless, insensitive, indiscriminate, amoral and impersonal material forces? Therapy? Even therapy, though helpful, contradicts itself within

---

[26] Paul M. Gould, *Cultural Apologetics: Renewing the Christian Voice, Conscience, and Imagination in a Disenchanted World* (Grand Rapids: Zondervan, 2019), 31.

[27] Richard Dawkins, *River Out of Eden: A Darwinian View of Life* (London: Basic Books, 1995), 133.

Humanism. Psychology is actually committed to understanding wrongdoing in a person's life, and then helping a person when a wrong has inflicted emotional pain. Therapeutic processes must acknowledge and operate on some implicit acknowledgement that arbitrarily diagnoses something having gone wrong and requiring a purposed restoration. Ultimately, humanity knows within itself that only something beyond itself can comfort and remedy the problem of evil, and so without God's resources it can be hopeless.

In *Finding God at Harvard*, a decades long distinguished physician and professor at Harvard Medical School wrote:

From my clinical observations and experiences, I cannot help but observe the very limited resources available to one with no faith and no hope. The lives of both Marx and Freud ended in bitterness and disillusionment. Though they experienced extensive hardship and adversity, they apparently lacked the spiritual resources to enable them to finish the course with any sense of hope. . . . Do the Scriptures promise freedom from adversity and pain? I do not think so. They make it clear that the world has been altered from its original state by our transgression of God's laws, and thus the world is filled with cruelty and suffering and war and sickness and death. But they also point out that the news is ultimately good, that there is cause for rejoicing. For we have been given great spiritual resources. . . . [28]

---

[28] Armand Nicholi, Jr., "Hope in a Secular Age" In *Finding God at Harvard*, Kelly Monroe, ed. (Grand Rapids: Zondervan, 1996), 111-120.

The "great spiritual resources" are found in Jesus who is the good news and who can forgive, provide inner healing, emotional comfort, and strength to overcome in a fallen world replete with evil. For He promises: "Come to Me, all you who labor and are heavy laden, and I will give you rest" (Matt. 11:28). His "rest" can comfort the inevitable agitations of evil and its emotional pain, and strengthen the inner person to cope with the vicissitudes of life. Faith in the Lord Jesus accepts the efficacy of God's grace, with an unmistakable sense of inner strength to endure hardship.

CF was illustrated by Jesus as capable of removing stumbling blocks as big as mountains from our lives. Jesus said authoritatively,

> Have faith in God, for assuredly I say to you whoever says to this mountain, Be removed and be cast into the sea, and does not doubt in his heart, but believes that those things he says will be done, he will have whatever he says (Mk. 11:23).

Let's appreciate what this often-quoted Scripture does not mean. Surely, it does not mean that God becomes our go to power to do whatever we wish anytime. God, make all those annoying colleagues resign. Done. Remove all competitors from my career path and then promote me at work. Done. Give me a big bonus so that I can buy a bigger house. Done. Make my flu go away now. Done. You get the point. God cannot be commanded to do whatever we wish, whenever we wish, regardless of how important we might deem the request. God is not a toy that is programmed to do whatever we wish.

What CF can expect is God's strength regardless of how monumental the stumbling blocks in our lives. Earnest pleas to God will always be satisfied with a profound sense of hope and comfort, though they may appear as "mountains." As the classic hymn describes the experience of countless Christians:

Great is Thy faithfulness. O God my Father,
There is no shadow of turning with Thee;
Thou changest not, Thy compassions, they fail not
As Thou hast been Thou forever wilt be.

Pardon for sin and a peace that endureth,
Thine own dear presence to cheer and to guide;
Strength for today and bright hope for tomorrow,
Blessings all mine, with ten thousand beside!

Great is Thy faithfulness....[29]

CF can also expect to receive heartfelt guidance from the Lord who revealed Himself as our "Good Shepherd" (Jn. 10:11). Believers can also expect to have their inner most being satisfied by the One who revealed Himself as "The Bread of Life" (Jn. 6:48). As a "branch," a Christian can expect to draw real life changing nourishment from the Christ who promised: "I am the vine, you are the branches. He who abides in Me, and I in him, bears much fruit; for without Me you can do nothing" (Jn. 15:5). CF's expectations are thus focused on a very real experience with an unfailing Saviour.

He guides, teaches, fulfills, and reveals a worldview far different from when you were outside CF. Your consciousness of

---

[29] Written by Thomas Chisholm (1866-1960), Music composed by William M. Runyan (1870-1957).

God rises, as well as your sense of values. Life becomes as John G. Stackhouse Jr. accurately described:

> Intellectually, one believes propositions one did not believe before. Morally, one has a different sense of what counts as good and evil, what one ought or ought not to do. Emotionally, one loves what one used to hate or ignore; one shuns former pleasures as toxic and wasteful. One cares about God, other people, the rest of the planet and oneself in a way one didn't before. Aesthetically, one finds beauty where one once saw nothing worthwhile at all, or perhaps even something repellant. Spiritually, one is sensitive and open to God, but also to the spiritual needs and gifts of other people. And one highly values the physical world, including one's body, as God's good creation.[30]

Thus, your perspective will often be contrary to the unregenerate mind expressed in culture. Values of CF thus become difficult to communicate for fear of rejection, or even embarrassment due to their unpopularity.

For example, the Good News of the Gospel was heralded by the announcement of the Saviour's birth: "you shall call His name JESUS, for He will save His people from their sins" (Matt. 1:21). Afterwards, Jesus began His ministry by proclaiming: "The time is fulfilled, and the kingdom of God is at hand. Repent, and believe in the gospel" (Mk 1:15). "Repent, and believe" in the Good News

---

[30] John G. Stackhouse, Jr. "What Conversion is and is not - Hint: It's not just about getting people saved," *Christianity Today* (Feb 2003): 70-75.

45

that now anyone's sins can receive forgiveness for free. Now if a Christian is to say to one's neighbour, "I have Good News for you. God can now forgive your sins for free. You can accept His grace by believing in the sacrifice of Jesus. It's good news!" This will surely cause an awkward moment, but that is the Gospel. Surely our communications require prudence and appropriate timing; but again, cultural thought considers such language as embarrassing, and it has influenced our ministries.

In today's culture, truth be told, we are being discouraged to point people to the Good News which requires repentance, because culture has grown in distaste for the language of CF and we know it. Seeker sensitive leaders are thus taking an approach that the Good News is all about people participating in the Kingdom of God ushered in by Jesus. Yes, but let us not try to trick people into the Kingdom of God. The truth is that repentance must first take place *before* one can participate in the Kingdom of God. Preaching repentance in our current culture will require wisdom, proper tonality, and surely, courage. Nevertheless, I was encouraged recently when I read a call to repentance and its power of freedom by a young Christian writer. In a "Spotlight on Culture," she wrote,

> Yeah, repent (a super unpopular word nowadays) but a powerful one nonetheless. When you repent for holding your plans above His, the idea doesn't hold you captive. Anxiety is replaced with peace; striving, with a sense of security and pleasure in the work you've been given. Like I said earlier, freedom blossoms. . . . Surrendering your life to His purpose

for your life is one of the most powerful things you can do. Trust me.[31]

The power of SC is in the communication of such themes as grace, repentance, redemption, fulfillment, and transformation, which remain applicable to humankind's brokenness observed all around us.

I believe the popularity of Jordan B. Peterson is due to people gravitating to how he has identified the reality of human brokenness, and has proposed a brand of instruction for them. He uses a knowledge of psychology to prescribe not *suggestions* for living, but necessary "rules for life." Peterson uses the term "chaos," which seems to substitute for the biblical understanding of humanity's fallenness, to describe humanity's challenges, pain, disappointments, failures, and ignorance. In *12 Rules for Life: An Antidote to Chaos,* Peterson writes:

> You may find that if you attend to these moral obligations, once you have placed 'make the world better' at the top of your value hierarchy, you experience ever-deepening meaning. It's not bliss. It's not happiness. It is something more like atonement for the criminal fact of your fractured and damaged Being. It's payment of the debt you owe for the insane and horrible miracle of your existence.[32]

---

[31] Katie Pezzutto, "Spotlight on Culture: When Your Life Looks Different Than You Expected," *Loving Is Moving: Canada's Christian Youth Magazine* (Jan/Feb 2019): Issue 31, 6.

[32] Jordan B. Peterson, *12 Rules For Life: An Antidote to Chaos* (Random House Canada, 2018), 200.

He appears to introduce a pseudo-religious manual that substitutes some of the classical language of Christianity with a contemporary secularized appeal. Cultural thought gravitates to secularized ideas that substitute Christianity and are presented by popular figures, especially those with credentials and success. If these *12 Rules for Life* were posited in a dissertation by an unknown doctoral candidate do you think they would have gained similar traction in culture? Why not? If rules for living are a serious antidote to a human predicament shouldn't they be respected regardless from where they came? Learning to discern content from hoopla surrounding cultural icons cannot be understated.

God Himself offers what everyone so desperately needs, love, grace and forgiveness. Accordingly, the depths of His grace remain indiscriminately applicable in all situations, even ones blocked by a "mountain." Kim Phuc Phan was the nine-year-old Vietnamese girl who was photographed in 1972 running naked on the roads of war-torn Vietnam. The captured image is widely known. Her clothes were burned off, and afterwards she underwent countless surgeries and spent over a year in the hospital, emerging with permanent physical and emotional scars. Recently, she was asked what she thought of war and the suffering it causes. This is what she replied:

> Steadying myself with a deep breath, I looked directly into the interviewer's eyes and said with quiet confidence, 'My position on this, and all matters, is *forgiveness*. My position, if you will, is *love*. My faith in Jesus Christ is what enabled me to forgive those who had wronged me - and as you know, the wrongs were severe. My faith in Jesus Christ is what enabled me to pray for my enemies rather than curse them. And my faith in Jesus

Christ is what enabled me to love them. I do not just tolerate them, nor am I merely civil toward them. No, I *love* them. It is this love alone that ends wars.' The woman, who had been very professional, very serious, very stoic at the beginning of our discussion, now had tears in her eyes. Several silent seconds passed before she cleared her throat and spoke: 'You are an amazing person,' she whispered to me.

'It is only the Lord,' I replied.[33]

We should all be brought to tears by this powerful testimony of God's grace within a believer. Mainstream culture would surely appreciate this interview and become impressed with Phuc Phan, but the narrative of love and forgiveness in Jesus are at best applaudable virtues and not meritorious in the true sense of SC. Forgiveness and genuine love towards perpetrators of pain and suffering, however, are not easy acts of general good will. Such an exercise of love during an experience of pain is nourished by what the Harvard doctor described as "great spiritual resources." By a genuine experience of the grace of God, coping with emotional pain and suffering, and being restored, becomes a real process that can console.

The most extreme of animosities can also be reconciled by the depths of God's love and grace in Jesus. Taysir "Tass" Abu Saada was born in Palestine and "trained as a sniper by Fatah to kill Jews,

---

[33] Kim Phuc Phan Thi, *Fire Road: The Napalm Girl's Journey through the Horrors of War to Faith, Forgiveness and Peace* (Carol Stream, Ill.: Tyndale Publishing House, 2017), 309-10.

he even instructed children about their duty to fight and kill Israelis."[34] Saada emigrated to the USA where he experienced conversion from Islam to Christianity. "During the same time period, God was working in the heart of an ex-Israeli soldier named Moran Rosenblit."[35] Rosenblit grew up in Israel with horrendous hatred towards Arabs, and fought as a soldier in Lebanon. Many of his friends were killed by Palestinian suicide bombers. He suffered with depression and abused alcohol. Then he emigrated to the USA and found Christ. As he says, "The light switch went on and from darkness I saw the light, and I accepted Jesus into my life."[36] Then Rosenblit was invited to speak at a conference for Jewish and Arab Christians. There he met Saada. The encounter is worth quoting at length. Rosenblit says,

> 'It was hard for me to share in front of Arab people . . . because some of those people might have . . . killed my friends.' As Moran finished . . . a Palestinian man approached him. 'I was a Fatah fighter' said . . . Saada, the . . . ex-PLO man. . . .
>
> 'I was in shock,' Moran recalls, as he . . . stared into Tass's eyes, trying to read his heart. Moran says Tass looked me in the eyes and he said, 'I love you.'
>
> 'I can't explain what that did to my heart when he said that.' Then Tass did something even more radical. 'He asked me to

---

[34] "Testimony of Two Friends: Love Replaces Hatred," Online, *http://jewishroots.net/library/testimonials/two_friends_testimony.html*

[35] Ibid.

[36] Ibid.

forgive him . . . for my friends who died from suicide bombers,' Moran says. 'It was God's grace that allowed me to forgive him,' he says. 'It was not my strength that I was able to forgive him.' Then Moran also sought forgiveness. 'I asked him to forgive me for not being able to love him and trust him and for my anger,' he says. 'And he did.' . . . Since that conference in March 2001, Moran and Tass speak to one another almost daily, as their bond of friendship grows without measure.

'Jesus touched my heart,' Tass says. 'It goes to show the world there is hope in Jesus.'[37]

Why do such accounts of reconciliation move us deeply? We are reminded powerfully of what we have tasted in CF, and how our spiritual lives are longing for a deeper relationship with God of which we are powerfully reminded.

Unfortunately, our experience of CF in North America has been impacted significantly by culture. We attend church, take our kids to Sunday school, engage in worship, listen to a sermon, give an offering, and then before the service has even concluded many have begun to scurry out of the sanctuary. Those who linger in the foyer quickly begin talking about politics, sports, food, business, automobiles, vacations, and some even compliment each other's fashion. Not that there is anything wrong with these conversations, but in the foyer of our churches our hearts are being revealed. If someone should ask a fellow believer in the foyer after the service, "What have you been learning from the Lord Jesus lately?" Many

---

[37] Ibid. Their dramatic story of love and forgiveness is also featured in the video *Forbidden Peace,* produced by *Jews for Jesus.*

would consider that question as weird. How can this be? In a church where moments ago we finished worshipping Jesus, where we made supplications, where He was proclaimed as the Saviour of the world! Where we gave of our hard-earned money to help promote discipleship. Could it be that our church experience has lost what was intended by SC? We are becoming what Jesus warned the traditional practices of His day: "These people draw near to Me with their mouth, And honour Me with their lips, But their heart is far from Me" (Matt. 15: 8-9). Please do not interpret this as a call to abandon how we are currently doing church. However, I am deeply concerned that our spiritual lives are now replacing an earnest pursuit of SC with formality of tradition, while secularism continues to affect us.

Each one of us, rather, should be pressing on to become a man or woman of God who can discern our times. Note the examples of how some Biblical characters, Joseph the son of Jacob, Moses, various Old Testament prophets, Ruth, Esther, Daniel, the Apostle Paul, were people who discerned their times. They were well educated, prudent in business, intellectual, and remarkably faithful to God. Even so, throughout history faithful Christians have been gifted scientists, mathematicians, lawyers, business people, and philosophers who all entered into a deeper experience of SC. In fact, many were ahead of their times. It has been written of John Wesley (1703-1791) that he was immersed "in classical culture." He had an "eager openness to 'modern' science and social change" with an "awareness of the entire Christian tradition as a living resource."[38] Further,

> His words and actions breathe the teachings, the imagery, the very vocabulary of Scripture. But his purpose was not to replicate the first century in eighteenth-century England, but rather to live in his own day a life that was faithful to the love that God had shown for humankind in Jesus Christ.[39]

Wesley's passion and deep experience of SC, with an awareness of the cultural thought of his day, engaged people effectively while remaining faithful to his convictions of CF. Let us follow the examples of those who went before us and effectively engaged their cultures. We should, therefore, endeavour "not to replicate the first century" in the twenty-first century, "but rather to live" in our times with an expression of the ageless message of SC.

Our efforts nowadays, though commendable, are nevertheless preoccupied with making the Gospel appear "cool." Now I do not intend to discourage innovative attempts at making the Gospel relevant so long as the teachings align with SC. We can learn something from Schaeffer who experienced deep Christian convictions and had a keen understanding of his culture. Interestingly, he encouraged "countercultural spirituality" by

---

[38] Thomas C. Oden, Leicester R. Longden, eds. *The Wesleyan Theological Heritage: Essays of Albert C. Outler* (Grand Rapids: Zondervan, 1991), 78.

[39] Richard P. Heitzenrater, *Wesley and the People Called Methodists* (Nashville: Abingdon Press, 1995), 318-19.

presenting the Gospel not as a "cool communication" but as a "hot communication":

> Schaeffer chooses to favour not the cool communication . . . but its opposite: 'I would like to reverse this. In a day of increasingly cool communication, biblical Christianity must make it very plain that it will deal only with hot communication. . . . It is a time for the church to insist, as a true revolutionary force, that there is truth.'[40]

Indeed, we must learn "to insist . . . that there is truth." We cannot desist from communicating the values of SC, and there is no other choice but to engage with contemporary culture. What I mean by engaging culture is trying to understand how people are now thinking, what trends are influencing them, what they desire and value, and then articulate how SC continues to provide meaningful and relevant answers to all areas of life.

SC remains foundational for a believer to discern the ideas, customs, and trends of cultural thought. It can open a believer's mind with a keener sense of how culture is *preferring* to think. Cultural thought borrows many values from SC while rejecting the relevancy of CF. It admires the principles of love, kindness, justice, mercy, and graciousness, and emphasizes their non-negotiability in society. When we realize how sensitive culture is to many Christian principles we will be better equipped to "insist" intelligently towards one step further, to the Gospel's power of grace to forgive,

---

[40] William Edgar, *Schaeffer on the Christian Life: Countercultural Spirituality* (Wheaton, Ill.: Crossway, 2013), 173.

restore, and fulfill. We can engage culture prudently and gently without negotiating any of the "true revolutionary force" of SC.

Behind SC we discover an infinite Mind. The Old Testament Scriptures foretold of Jesus, and centuries later the New Testament recorded the fulfillment of those earlier prophecies. The New Testament writers also explained the human experience of sin, repentance, grace, and redemption, which subsequent generations have also likewise experienced. Today we experience grace and spiritual rebirth identically as was described by the writers of SC. Altogether one cannot reasonably believe that the Bible was all a human invention by forty authors over a span of about 1400 years, most of whom never met each other. It wasn't humanly possible for each century to piggyback on the previous one, and intentionally manage the novel to keep the canard flourishing. If one were to read the Scriptures open-mindedly, one would reasonably conclude that CF must have come from God and not from a collective conspiratorial agreement among generations to keep the fantasy alive. One may not like what SC concludes, or wish to follow SC, but one could not reasonably accept that the Scriptures were a human fabrication. "Knowing this first," wrote the Apostle Peter centuries after the Old Testament writers and after witnessing the life of Jesus, "that no prophecy of scripture is of any private interpretation, for prophecy never came by the will of man" (2 Pet. 1:20). Skeptics read a portion of Scripture here, and a portion of Scripture there, and pounce with intense focus on the minor discrepancies. They do not want any of it to be true. They feel it is too constraining to submit to the Lord Jesus and follow all His regressive requirements, and so they proffer a claim that He is irrelevant and unrelatable to contemporary people. That is where cultural thought is at; and while Christians experience the beauty and fulfillment of SC, their tension with culture is becoming spiritually stressful.

Now I encourage you to read the following without any cultural filters. Pause, and try hard to imagine what an Ephesian Christian would have experienced when this passage was heard for the very first time:

> that Christ may dwell in your hearts through faith; that you, being rooted and grounded in love, may be able to comprehend with all the saints what is the width and length and depth and height - to know the love of Christ which passes knowledge; that you may be filled with all the fullness of God. now to Him who is able to do exceedingly abundantly above all that we ask or think, according to the power that works in us, to Him be glory in the church by Christ Jesus to all generations . . . (Eph. 3: 17-21).

Wasn't that different? Wasn't it Scripturally refreshing? "Jesus to *all generations*"! In Christ, you must come to a deep realization that God has placed something special within you, and that you now see "this generation" of culture from a very real perspective of grace. I believe we can grow to where we no longer have it in us anymore to exercise unbelief, because our *knowingness* of SC will provide *real* substance and remind us of where we came from, what the Lord has made of us, and where would we be today without Jesus?

So how can believers live out their CF with *knowingness*? Next chapter, I will discuss the necessity of prioritizing "the one thing needed." Is your hunger for God deep? Are you thirsting for Him? God also promises, "Call to Me, and I will answer you, and show you great and mighty things, which you do not know" (Jer. 33:3). I would politely ask in return: Are you ready to commit? You should also know that such a commitment will definitely cost you something. It's not that you will be required to live in solitude until God thunders unmistakably into your life. That stereotype should not be associated with the deeper things of God. Neither is the implication here that you will have to perform spiritual exercises "twenty-four, seven." A lively relationship with God, however, does entail a readiness to engage with spiritual battles. In other words, "It is a fearful thing to fall in the hands of the living God" (Heb. 10:31). A triumphant and fulfilling CF is attainable, if you open your heart and mind *while not being intimidated by the denigrations of cultural thought.*

So then, is there anything ensnaring you and keeping you back from a deeper walk with our Lord Jesus?

Chapter 2

SCRIPTURAL REFRESH AND THE "ONE THING NEEDED"

"Martha, Martha, you are worried and troubled about many things. But one thing is needed, and Mary has chosen that good part, which will not be taken away from her" Luke 10:41

In North America, the distractions keeping believers from a deeper CF have clearly become the comforts of material things. Moreover, in Toronto where I reside, many church buildings are being converted to condo buildings. It has become a phenomenon. What is going on? In a sea of material distractions, large screen televisions, the internet and its endless clicks of entertainment, increasing access to fancy cars and vacations, an obsession with home renovations, dining out more often, and living in an unprecedented era of prosperity, we have wandered into an irresistible *comfort zone*. As a Christian, would you like to know something? The allure of material things is not going away anytime soon. Would you like to know something else? Neither is SC going away. The fate of humankind is inherently linked to God. "I am the Alpha and the Omega, the beginning and the end, says the Lord, who is and who was and who is to come, the Almighty" (Rev. 1:8). Material requirements have become an integral part of our lives, and although they are causing much distraction from our Lord, they are not intrinsically bad. Many believers even desire to do more for the less fortunate, but are distracted in the comfort zone. Yet the seed of CF within us continues to whisper for spiritual nourishment. What are we to do?

Not too long-ago Christians attended church twice on Sundays, and consistently met during the week for prayer and Bible study. Conversations with one another about CF were common and enjoyable. They experienced together what it was like to have "obtained like precious faith" (2 Pet. 1:2). Their fellowships occupied a central spot in their lives. Now if you are thinking that those poor people were stuck in a legalistic lifestyle, I invite you to think again. Legalism is a term showing up today in Christian circles like advert banners on our social media pages. So let's begin by acknowledging what *will not* contribute to a deeper CF. The longstanding allusion to Jesus's blasting of Pharisaical practices in Matthew 23 has now taken on the meaning that we are not to base our CF on laws of do's and don'ts, because we are partakers of God's grace.

Basically, legalism is a belief that following certain moral practices will earn you favour with God and not following them will warrant His disfavour. Legalism is false because there are no rules or moral codes which a human being can observe in order to earn reconciliation with God. Isaiah well noted when juxtaposing human works with God: "we are all like an unclean thing and all our righteousness are like filthy rags" (Is. 64:6). Only the grace of God as revealed in Jesus's teaching, death and resurrection, accepted by faith, will place us in a favourable position with God. "For by grace you have been saved through faith, and that not of yourselves; it is the gift of God, not of works, lest anyone should boast" (Eph. 2:8-9).

The issue, however, is that when believers consider an action which is not explicitly forbidden in Scripture, like drinking cognac or buying lottery tickets, those who partake label the objectors as legalists. Christians on both sides can have equally strong moral convictions, and each can marshal an argument in favour of their particular choice. With all fairness, sometimes Christians who choose not to indulge truly have no desire to do so. It's not that they believe abstaining will score points with God or that partaking will warrant His displeasure. Personally, I do believe that the Spirit can reveal God's will for each one of us concerning such actions. Jesus did promise, "when He, the Spirit of truth, has come, He will guide you into all truth" (Jn. 16:13). So "whether you eat or drink, or whatever you do, do to the glory of God" (1 Cor. 10:31). The Spirit can "guide" us towards "the glory of God," and I will illustrate with a true story.

I knew a young man who had been meeting with his childhood friends every Friday evening since high school to play poker for money. By early twenties, they had already established themselves with good jobs and some ran promising businesses. During that time, this young man became a Christian. The following Friday he attended their usual poker meeting, but he hesitated to sit down at the regular spot reserved for him. His friends noticed that there was something peculiar about him that evening. They encouraged him to take a seat at the table. He refused, and bashfully shared that he had become a Christian and was thus uncomfortable playing for money. As you can imagine, they sneered and mocked while trying to remain polite. Then they mentioned how he was already a Christian and accustomed to going to confession on Saturdays with them since they were kids. They would go and confess their sins, perform penance, and receive forgiveness from God. Then they would start fresh, and the following week go again, confess, and perform penance. This young man explained how there was no need for that anymore, because Jesus had paid the price for our sins once and for all and He alone provided a personal relationship with God. Then they insisted that he should forget about this religious stuff and sit down and play.

He told them that he had no desire to play. Without any theological training, he began to explain how he had lost the craving and that he felt it was not right that they should compete for each other's money. He explained further that they all earned their money working and so they should not covet to take it away from one another. He also emphasized that playing poker didn't appeal to him anymore. He remained for a few minutes and then left. The following week he did not show up. After a few weeks of absences, he got a phone call from one of his friends, inquiring where he had been. He mentioned that he was attending a young people's group on Friday evenings at his new church. His friend commented that this religious thing would last another week or two and then he would surely return. Decades later they still keep in touch and his friends have acknowledged the work of God's grace in his life.

Deciding not to play poker for money was not a legalistic decision; simply put, there was no desire to play anymore. He had new desires and felt satisfied that his decision was made "to the glory of God." If you are still convinced that the young man's decision was legalistic then I would ask you politely to think about something. There are no right or wrong answers; only a few questions that will hopefully inform you by your own introspection. Seriously, are you bored with your CF? Is your CF providing you with real satisfaction, "with joy inexpressible and full of glory" (1 Pet. 1:8)? Do you "delight yourself also in the Lord" (Ps. 37:4)? Do you feel that your desires must fit into your CF regardless of the convictions of fellow believers? Do you find that obeying SC - yes there are commands - too burdensome? Jesus *commanded* us to, "First remove the plank from your own eye, and then you will see clearly to remove the speck from your brother's eye" (Matt. 7:5).

So before loosely using that term, legalism, one should think it through carefully. We should appreciate that fellow believers are participating in the grace of God and they truly enjoy not indulging in what others are sometimes doing. Surely you agree that criticizing does no good whatsoever to one's CF? Being adamant usually makes one side, or both, bolster up their perspective and thereby creating schisms among Christian relationships. Paul taught us in Romans: ". . . nor do anything by which your brother stumbles or is offended or is made weak. . .. Let each of us please his neighbor for his good, leading to edification" (14:21; 15:2). We are to avoid moral and ministerial competitions, encourage one another in the grace of God, and let the Spirit teach us.

I also find that some believers who grew up in Christian homes think that their upbringing had imposed killjoy rules on them, and now as adults they feel resentful. Some are contemporary Christian leaders who sometimes lightly mock their heritages, or push the envelope on traditional evangelical beliefs, because they feel the teachings were legalistic, and now they know better. I can understand the occasional frustration, but aren't we required by our Lord Jesus to forgive and not hold grudges? C. S. Lewis captured it brilliantly when he said, "Everyone says forgiveness is a lovely idea, until they have something to forgive."[41] Why not appreciate something that your Christian heritage got right for raising you to where you are today? Regardless of how or when we came to saving faith, each one ought to grow securely now in their CF and "stand fast . . . in the liberty by which Christ has made us free" (Gal. 5:1). Above all, Jesus said authoritatively: "A new commandment I give to you, that you love one another; as I have loved you, that you also love one another" (Jn. 13:34). If you are not loving *all* your brothers and sisters in Christ, as commanded by the Master, then I will leave it up to you to interpret what that is saying about your CF. Lest I be accused of judging.

Now I may be reprimanded here by some church leaders, but the belief that tithing or giving big offerings will enrich your CF is misleading. Indeed, we are under Scriptural injunction to "give, and it will be given to you" (Lk 6:38). Nonetheless Jesus was not referring strictly to the giving of money. Christians should "give" of their time, share their resources happily, sometimes helping the less fortunate pro bono, as well as giving monetarily. When you thus "give" you will then receive enormous spiritual dividends and favourable treatment in return, and not necessarily blessings of monetary value. When you do give monetarily be sure to do so "not grudgingly or of necessity; for God loves a cheerful giver" (2 Cor. 9:7). You should give because you enjoy doing so wholeheartedly, and not because you feel constrained, or guilty if you don't. In my understanding, you are better off giving within

---

[41] Manser, *The Westminster Collection of Christian Quotations*, 114.

63

your threshold of cheerfulness, however little or big it may be, rather than tithing "grudgingly." Your priority should be to deepen your relationship with Jesus, and then you will become happier and more effective all around.

Furthermore, taking on roles of leadership in the church will not deepen your CF. In fact, spiritually malnourished leaders are susceptible to regressing to the shallow end of CF, because they are like Martha who neglected "that good part." She wanted to minister but was not focusing on "the one thing needed," that is, Jesus. Martha was distracted with serving, and neglected the priority of first learning at the feet of Jesus. Today there is too much focus on Christian leadership without the priority of knowing Him. Likewise, there is enormous pressure to be an effective Christian leader and *lead, lead, lead,* while the necessary inward strength of Jesus is being neglected. Mary, on the other hand, went immediately to the feet of Jesus when He entered her house and submitted herself to Him. Christian leaders are "worried and troubled" with their professional roles, and thus turning to literature on leadership, attending seminars on leadership, and gobbling up anything that they believe will make them successful.

For those leading a Sunday school class, a Bible study, a prayer meeting, or a small group, neither will these in and of themselves provide a deeper CF. Leadership is intended to communicate and to encourage believers towards a deeper CF by those who have already experienced it to a significant degree. Otherwise, as Jesus said: "They are blind leaders of the blind. And if the blind leads the blind, both will fall into a ditch" (Matt. 15:14). Inevitably, frustrations loom for everyone when leaders have not yet been at the feet of Jesus and learned of "that good part." But here is the kicker: our North American Christian model of ministry is set-up so that the prestigious roles are in leadership, as they receive more attention and respect. Nowadays Christian leaders are made to feel as miniature celebrities in their respective circles. The attention can become intoxicating, especially in bigger churches where even a lay leader can oversee hundreds. The fanfare is battling the Spirit's inner working of deepening Christ like humility and selflessness.

Sure, there are many spiritually strong pastoral and lay leader teams that work diligently to serve, and are deepening their own CF with a keen understanding of SC. Such leaders are serving with an ongoing realization that they are Christians first and ministers second, and not the other way around. Christian leaders must exercise a calling of God by prioritizing Jesus first, and leading second. They must know the behavioural distinctives of a Mary from a Martha before Jesus, because the authority and prestige of leadership can often seduce a leader into an *assumed* position of deep CF. Both Martha and Mary were in the company of Jesus, but it was Mary who knew "the one thing needed." Followers of Jesus are hungering to know God, and we must get "that good part" which is indispensable to great Christian leadership. In addition, Christian leaders are pressured to achieve their ministry's metrics, financial obligations, and juggle the needs of their own families. The vulnerability is to take on SC as a daily professional routine, overlooking "that good part" required to advance a greater presence of God in the lives of everyone. Nonetheless if you still believe that a role in Christian leadership is tantamount to a deep CF you should earnestly study and seek to understand why Mary planted herself at the feet of Jesus. What is the nature of "that good part"?

Jesus said, "Learn from me, for I am gentle and lowly in heart, and you will find rest for your souls" (Matt. 11:29). To truly "learn from" Jesus is to become increasingly "gentle and lowly in heart." This is deep. This is real power for all followers of Jesus. Only Jesus Himself can provide the spiritual strength, lively relationship with God, and genuine humility required to place the interests of others before our own. This is the making of a true servant leader. To know what it really means to "let nothing be done through selfish ambition or conceit, but in lowliness of mind let each esteem others better than himself" (Phil. 2:3). In reference to this passage, a Pastor in North Carolina wrote, "I cannot help but believe that if pastors emblazoned those verses in their mind's eye to be reviewed and practiced daily, the state of our churches would be significantly different."[42] However, this is a path of most resistance. In a time where an aura of special status surrounds a position in church leadership it is extremely painful to "choose" to do what Mary did and humble oneself at the feet of Jesus. Now again, there are plenty of solid church leaders who are sacrificial, good students of SC, commendable family people, significant contributors in ministry, and have a growing relationship with Jesus. Nevertheless, the path to a deeper CF is doubly challenging for those who serve in leadership roles. The path of least resistance is to become like Martha and minister about without painfully bowing down at the feet of the Master.

---

[42] David Horner, *A Practical Guide for Life and Ministry: Overcoming 7 Challenges Pastors Face* (Grand Rapids: Baker Books, 2008), 121-22.

For all roles, ministry today in North America is increasingly challenging even in the best of situations. Funds are tight, with a glut of well qualified candidates. An opening for a paid position in an evangelical ministry could easily attract a hundred qualified applicants. The employed are then mandated with clear expectations and deliverables. Metrics are largely based on either numerical growth or increasing donations. If more and more people are drawn, or giving, then the leaders are doing a fine job. This fixation is causing enormous stress on employed Christian leaders as they diligently try to deliver, with trepidation of otherwise being replaced. Bear in mind that they have families to support, and the cost of living in major North American cities is barely manageable. The boards of ministries consist mainly of accomplished business people who are all decent people, but their expectations are strictly borne from their own business successes. In consequence, the quest to promote a deeper CF and understanding of SC is falling through the cracks of our structures. While employed Christian leaders are busy and stressed with the *business of ministry* the priority shifts away from pursuing a deeper relationship with Jesus. Consequently, there is too much of "Martha" going on, and not enough of "Mary."

Seminaries are now offering graduate degrees on Christian leadership. In my inbox, I received an advertisement touting a master's degree program which will assure the graduate of becoming a successful leader. This program will teach a student how to market effectively, because the underlying assumption is that today in ministry a leader must compete for people's donations. It lists that a student will be educated in finance and fundraising principles. The program will also train on how to have maximum impact on people as a Christian leader. After all, prospective Christian employers are now expecting their leaders to coach staff in order to achieve objectives. Prospective students are also promised an in-depth study of theology that will enrich their ministries. Not only so, but they will be equipped to lead in any cultural context. Thus, the subtle pitch to appeal to prospective foreign students who wish to be educated in North America, because here we have a track record for producing Christian superstars. The program facilitators obviously base the curriculum on the *assumption* that applicants already have a deep CF and a good working knowledge of SC. This assumption, however, is a colossal misjudgment. What the program will produce is graduates who will be compelled to concentrate on themselves, rather than on Jesus. Humility will not be fundamental, because the mind has been filled with ways on how to compete and succeed in the marketplace of ministry. Surely Christian employers will expect someone with a master's degree in Christian leadership to be distinguished and trained to apply proven theories. How else would they lead and drive results?

Accordingly, instruction on coaching and mentoring followers will be part of the curriculum, but leaders will also graduate with a mindset to go and accomplish their own professional objectives. This is an altogether different strategy from leading people to a deeper relationship with Jesus for effective discipleship. The program should really be offering a course on what it means to be a Scriptural leader, and then discuss each other's learnings with classmates. Perhaps a whole course should be dedicated to learning about one of the greatest leaders of all time "(Now the man Moses, was very humble, more than all men who were on the face of the earth)" (Num. 12:3). Another course should assign leadership exercises within local community initiatives where the life changing power of the Gospel is desperately needed. Then students can take turns leading the class on their learnings, and the instructor provides evaluation with Scriptural input. A required course also on the pitfalls of leadership and the devastating consequences they can wreak on the family of God, for cultural thought is always quick to capitalize on the sins of Christian leaders. Many case studies are available to learn from in our history of Christian leadership. Then the student should be required to produce a thesis on what are the Scriptural motives for leadership, and how to fulfill them.

Of course, the problem with the foregoing is the lack of glamour. Even so, a master's degree in servanthood would be a lesser draw and probably lead to the program's insolvency. Christian leadership has been so highly touted to the point that it has taken on a stereotypical character that seeks to establish a perception of being God's man or woman. This is the draw. Many want to identify with the prestige of being God's person and be admired as such by everyone else.

The challenge is that many believers who are gripped by material distractions, and tempted to live in the comfort zone, are also looking to their leaders for spiritual guidance. Material comforts are offering tempting satisfiers, and we need leaders who will be mandated to lead believers towards experiencing the deep inner fulfillment of SC. The cultural pull of material things on believers cannot be addressed effectively by leaders who are trained, and then pressured, to achieve numerical and financial success. Meanwhile, the "self-fulfillment" found in culture is creeping in to substitute for the abundant life Jesus promised (John 10:10). Note this cultural predicament as described in *Good Faith*:

> Too many Christians have substituted comfortable living for a life changed by the gospel. . .. the morality of self-fulfillment has begun to bear its inevitable fruit: people want to fulfill themselves by doing things outside the bounds of cultural Christianity. . .. Nearly everything about the broader culture is expertly marketed to appeal to our comfort, well-being, safety, and satisfaction. A delicious meal. Your dream holiday. The perfect house. Great sex. What will fulfill you?[43]

Clearly, CF is currently not satisfying enough to overcome the temptations of its material competitors in "the broader culture." I strongly believe that we must discern these cultural times and begin to rearrange our priorities. Christian leadership must reorient itself and realize what it's truly called of God to accomplish. Otherwise, I think that many believers will end up playing church and going through life missing out on the real fulfillment of SC and failing to make a difference in our cultural times. How is this all going to change so that more believers discipline themselves and begin to enjoy a bit more of what really matters in life?

The words of Jesus expressed a mind that was intent on shedding light in a world of darkness. Daily, we can observe this world's darkness: victims of poverty, violence, sexual exploitation, drugs, floods, forest fires, mental and emotional challenges, race

---

[43] David Kinnaman and Gabe Lyons, *Good Faith: Being a Christian When Society Thinks You're Irrelevant and Extreme* (Grand Rapids: Baker Books, 2016), 59, 61.

tensions, senseless shootings, and please forgive me if I missed anything that has impacted you. Even our history books reveal darkness upon darkness in each bygone age. His light was intended to brighten the lives of people in every generation and to provide power to transition from darkness to making an impact in our societies. How many times have we witnessed His power of grace in the lives of redeemed people who then impacted society?

Throughout history SC has founded and developed prestigious universities, medical centres, benevolent societies, and impacted community initiatives. Previously, we learned from some powerful testimonies how only Jesus could have accomplished such drastic transformations from animus to genuine love, from hurt to forgiveness, and from darkness to light. The mind of Christ revealed a knowledge of humanity's most inner struggles and need of grace, and then He sacrificed His own life to provide the solution for our wickedness and wretchedness. Accordingly, it was an appropriate reaction from his listeners when after He finished His great Sermon on the Mount "that the people were astonished at His teaching" (Matt. 7:28). Jesus had no ulterior motives. His words expressed a mind of utmost selflessness and sincere compassion for His followers. He now invites us to participate in a wonderful relationship with Him so that we can become bearers of His "light."

Deepening our relationship with Jesus must be *intentional*. As Dallas Willard (1935-2013) taught us, "In the heart of a disciple there is a . . . *settled intent*. Having come to some understanding of what it means, and thus having 'counted the costs,' the disciple of

Christ desires above all else to be like him."[44] First, we ought to remind ourselves that as followers of Christ it was, He who invited us. "My sheep hear my voice," said Jesus, "and I know them, and they follow me" (Jn. 10:27). We must know who is *He* that has invited *us*. Entering into a deep relationship with Jesus begins with "intently" acknowledging the call.

Excuses of busyness today have become tyrannical. It is customary now to book an appointment with a friend a week in advance in order to meet for coffee, with multiple flips of texts and emails negotiating dates and times. What has become of us? We have plenty of time for social media, for fooling around on the internet, and watching movies and sports events. There is even a new term for it, "binge watching," where countless hours are spent consecutively viewing an entertainment program. Not to mention time spent writing and evaluating online the services we received. People even spend hours lining up for event tickets, for early bird discounts on things, and for the hope of being one of the first to buy a newly released gadget. We even have more time off than previous generations as employers are now providing more vacation time, floater days, personal days, and maternal/paternal time off. Professors and teachers get sabbaticals and summers off. Students also have plenty of breaks and summers off. It's not that we have become too busy. That is a myth. What we value with our time has changed dramatically. It's more accurate to say that we have become way too distracted, and careless with our use of time.

---

[44] Dallas Willard, *The Great Omission* (San Francisco: Harper, 2006), 7. The italics are mine.

Now it is true that North American life has become far more competitive and we need to work harder, study harder, and spend resources preparing our children for their utmost potential. Yet social media and internet surfing have become priorities and many have an addiction to their smart phone, which all become time consuming activities that create this artificial belief of busyness. No wonder that such dependency is causing us to crave actual fellowship with people less and less, and affecting other aspects of our lives. A friend of our family teaches third grade and over lunch mentioned that a colleague asked if she would watch over her class. Our friend's colleague had forgotten her smart phone at home and had to leave her class to go pick it up. Unbelievable! How much time does a school teacher have during the day outside the class that could be spent on a smart phone? The fact of the matter is that people can no longer see themselves living without their smart phones. All of our free time is quickly distracted by screens, and their value have become quite high in our lives. This supposed sense of busyness is enslaving Christians and robbing them from pursuing what really matters in life. We must exercise deliberate intention to exit this comfort zone. A determination is required to discover what Jesus accomplished for us, and to satisfy our hunger for *real fulfillment and knowingness*. Ironically, it takes much more effort to spend hours binge watching programs and being nosy about everyone else's life on social media than to adjust one's lifestyle to include quality time for SC. Such activities, however, have become a high personal value for believers and causing them to think they are too busy to prioritize their CF.

Can we realistically disconnect our devices? No, we cannot. Interestingly enough, however, a while ago my wife and I decided to disconnect our internet access at home for one month. Our family then spent more time together, riding our bikes, going to the library, going for walks and hikes, and reading more. Homework activity also increased; conversation increased; mealtimes were not rushed; there was a palpable sense of increased collaboration in our household. We were all visibly more relaxed. I am not recommending that all Christian families attempt this one-month exercise. At the time, our son was thirteen years old; it was easier to implement. If you have older teenagers, or young adults, such an internet fast could backfire. It could create more tension within your family. Nevertheless, if everyone agreed to it then it might be an exercise worth pursuing, even if it only lasts for one or two days, or an evening. Everyone will surely learn something from the exercise. If it is you and your spouse, or you live alone, then try an exercise of turning the internet off for an evening or two, or a weekend, or a week, or for as long you can bear. You will surely emerge having learned quite a bit about what really matters in life as opposed to what doesn't amount to much.

Discipline will be the main factor in your pursuit of SC, and your refresh must begin where your CF began, with Jesus Himself. Regardless of where you are now with your walk with Jesus you can begin to go deeper. He once asked a question to specific listeners after which no one dared "question Him anymore" (Matt. 22:45). Jesus had asked, "What do you think about the Christ?" (Matt. 22:42). The answer one gives determines a great deal for that individual's life and faith. What was yours when you first heard it? Is He truly the Saviour of the world who offers something special to a believer, and extraordinarily unlike anything else in our short lives? You are a Christian, and intently exploring the answer to the ultimate question of Jesus will supersede any of the culture's suggestions for fulfillment. Pursuing SC should be an indispensable value on your ongoing "to do list." Jesus will encourage you, "Let not your heart be troubled; you believe in God, believe also in me" (Jn. 14:1).

Preachers who present a shallow brand of Christianity with emphasis on being saved, dying, and going to heaven, should deepen their own experience and understanding of SC. The teaching is true, but the emphasis should be on what Jesus taught about our CF in the here and now: "But seek first the kingdom of God and its righteousness" (Matt. 6:33). "For indeed, the kingdom of God is within you" (Lk. 17:21). Begin by carving out a small portion of your time and explore "the kingdom of God within you." The next time you are having coffee with your smart phone in hand why not study a portion of Scripture rather than spending all your time playing a game? Intentionally dig into "the kingdom of God" with confidence that you will discover a deeper relationship with Jesus. Again, "Let not your heart be troubled."

Now note that when it comes to Scriptural study it's the quality of reading that will deepen your CF. Dismiss the thought immediately that the Scriptures are too difficult to comprehend. Dismiss also the thought that they lack excitement. Scriptures are read and truths are conveyed unlike any other literature. They will reveal deeper meanings about humankind, about you, your family, relationships, career, and most of all your relationship with Jesus. You can surely dismiss cultural thought's misinformed opinion that the Scriptures are no longer relevant. A reading, or rather an intentional study, of Scripture must be careful and with complete concentration. It's quite normal to read a passage numerous times before the light goes on in your mind. There will be many extraordinary propositions which are initially difficult to understand, but be patient and even seek explanatory resources.[45] Why not spend less money on entertainment and a bit more on discovering the depths of SC? With deliberate focus, you should endeavour to allow the text to speak for itself. There will be plenty that require multiple readings; this is also quite normal.

You must be open to allowing the Scriptures to inform your mind and to work inside of you. Some of the greatest Christian minds have been challenged and shaped by Scripture. A helpful commentary here by a notable British theologian, John Stott (1921-2011), states that,

> If we come to Scripture with our minds made up, expecting to hear from it only an echo of our own thoughts and never the thunderclap of God's, then indeed he will not speak to us and we shall only be confirmed in our own prejudices. We must allow the Word of God to confront us, to disturb our security, to undermine our complacency and to overthrow our patterns of thought and behavior.[46]

Allow yourself gradual increments of Scriptural comprehension by an openness to what God wishes to teach you, and behold how the Spirit will fulfill your inner longings. Unmistakably, a genuine

---

[45] You should invest in commentaries. They will teach you and make your personal study of Scripture increasingly enjoyable. Commentaries are not reserved for preachers and teachers. Every Christian should own multiple commentaries.

[46] Manser, *The Westminster Collection of Christian Quotations*, 19.

intent to understand the revelation of God in Scripture will yield life changing experiences.

When you met Jesus, you would have gone through "the Door." For He said, "I am the door. If anyone enters by me, he will be saved, and will go in and out and find pasture" (Jn. 10:9). What does His revelation of "The Door" mean to you? You should know that once you enter in you are not stuck there, for Jesus also said that you "will go *in and out*." Each time you exit, however, you will not be the same as when you entered. Jesus described Himself as "the Door" because a door is an entrance from one spot to another designated place. An observation here is that even in Jesus's time a door had a peephole, or perhaps even cracks. The point is that looking through a door's peephole or cracks and observing what is on the other side is not the same as walking through the door and entering into the other side. Today, you can walk by glass doors and see people enjoying dinner on white table cloths, but it's a completely different matter to go in, sit down, order from the menu, enjoy the service, eat the well-presented and delicious food, and then leave with a fine dining experience. You're beginning to get the point. Many today are looking at Jesus through the peephole, through the cracks of the door, through the glass, but are not going "in and out" and "finding pasture." SC is indeed alive and available to you today and it can provide a deeper relationship with Jesus, if you will be open, make time to reflect, and apply yourself to learn what it means to enter the "Door."

When we get hungry a meal is required to satisfy ourselves and to make us feel better, and function optimally. In like manner, humanity has an ongoing hunger for inner fulfillment, and if believers are not being fulfilled by Jesus then sinful temptations lurk everywhere outside "The Door." Jesus knew of our inner longings for fulfillment, and so He commended Mary for prioritizing "that good part," while He sought to teach Martha likewise. Mary prioritized time for Jesus, whereas Martha gave priority to other tasks and became distracted from her Master. Can you imagine the Saviour of the world in your house and you not prioritizing to first be with Him? Surely, she would have fellowshipped with Jesus *afterwards*. He is in your life today and I encourage you to choose to seek first "the one thing needed." Without Him, we cannot be completely happy in CF, and if we are not growing in the "grace and knowledge of our Lord and Saviour" (2 Pet. 3:18) then we will be more susceptible to sinful fulfilments. Scripture teaches abundantly on how sin cannot provide the real fulfillment we desire, especially when we have known Christ.

After David's adulterous affair with Bathsheba and her impregnation, and his murderous conspiracy to kill her husband Uriah (2 Sam. 11), he not only destroyed her family but his also crumbled. Amnon, a son of David and half-brother to Tamar a daughter of David, lusted after her with unquenchable desire (2 Sam. 13). He then pretended to be ill and arranged for her to serve him a meal privately. When they were alone, he raped her. "Then Amnon hated her exceedingly, so that the hatred with which he hated her was greater than the love with which he had for her. And Amnon said to her, 'Arise, be gone!'" (2 Sam. 13:15). I remember when I read this for the first-time decades ago that I was literally brought to tears for Tamar. Everyone should be brought to tears for her. Amnon behaved demonically. As a human being, he experienced an inner feeling of emptiness and her beautiful innocence became an immediate reminder to him of his moral turpitude. The cravings for sinful fulfillment can be very strong, and all human beings are susceptible to them, as were David and Amnon. Sin has consequences, however, and can spiral our lives out of control, affecting our loved ones. Tamar continues to remind us of how sin can devastate innocent lives and exploit the vulnerable. As believers, we should continually be vigilant with all of our resources to prevent such violations of people.

No matter how broken we may feel about our relationship with God we can be restored, and so can everyone around us. The intentional purpose of SC is to provide life changing grace to all those who admit to its requirement: "If we confess our sins, He is faithful and just to forgive us our sins and to cleanse us from all unrighteousness" (1 Jn. 1:9). Sin is the problem in our world, and it is a destructive force. It can shatter one's relationships, one's family, and emotions to countless pieces. God intends for us to realize that sin has enormous consequences in our lives and relationships. So "where sin abounded, grace abounded much more" (Rom. 5:20). The intentional purpose of SC is for the grace of God to "abound" in our lives, not in theoretical ways but in very *real ways*. When we are tempted to engage in sin and destructive behaviour we should know how to rely on His inner strength to overcome.

Why should we seek the grace of God and overcome? What is the point of continuing to "fight the good fight of faith" and overcome the struggle with things that everyone else is doing anyways? Why not seek pleasure as encouraged to do so by cultural thought? After all, as long as you aren't hurting anyone isn't transgression fun and CF boring? Have you ever thought of that?

Several years ago, my fellow theologues and I heard about how a famous movie star had referred to sin as fun. The actor was asked about his reckless behaviour after arriving in Hollywood, and with a smirk he replied that he thought sin was fun. Everyone laughed. Some of you are probably laughing too, and thinking that's so funny, and some are probably thinking that's so cool. I submit to you that the initial impression of the reply can elicit a laugh, but as Christians we should find it utterly selfish and inconsiderate. At the time, my friends and I discussed his answer theologically, and wondered how as Christians we would have replied to such an answer?

First of all, we would have pointed out how driving a Ferrari at full speed while intoxicated can easily kill you or leave you as a paraplegic, and possibly do the same to others on the road. That isn't fun or cool at all. Furthermore, such a tragedy would cause so much pain to one's family and friends, with devastation to others as well. That isn't funny or cool either. Likewise, drinking alcohol excessively and doing drugs can wreak havoc on your health, your relationships, your loved ones, and your integrity as a gifted human being. Is all that still fun? Your promiscuity is also increasing the likelihood of disease, of emotional pains to you and others, and feelings of frustration and betrayal. Should you disregard this advice and continue to party on then doesn't it reveal utter selfishness for yourself and inconsideration for everyone else? How can you then experience genuine love and fulfillment when you continue on with total disregard for everyone? This counsel is coming from those who love you and care about your well-being. We don't want you or your family and friends to suffer immense pain, which really is inevitable on this course.

After providing the foregoing counsel, with genuine concern, love and courteousness, we would have explained how all of us are tempted to fulfill our lives outside of God's intended design for fulfillment. He is not requesting that you give up anything that is good for you and others, only what is bad. Jesus provides grace, inner fulfillment, and an abundant life unlike anything else. Unless one is living the abundant life that Jesus promised by the power of God's grace then the need for ultimate contentment will continue to engage in selfish behaviour. Some of you might think that was a lame answer. That is okay. You would have to agree, however, that human selfishness is not virtuous; neither is complete inconsideration for one's friends and family; likewise care and love for people is commendable. We were going one step further and presenting the Gospel to someone who is the object of God's love and grace, and leaving it up to the Spirit to do its business. "Oh, taste and see that the Lord is good; Blessed is the man that trusts in Him" (Ps. 34:8)!

Nowadays the cravings for what will make one feel good have intensified in culture. Humanity's quest is for a measure of fun in almost everything it does, and it seeks to be free from all moral impositions which forbid pleasure. SC has thus become unpopular, not necessarily because it's deemed irrelevant, but more so that it's perceived as too restrictive to "feel good" pursuits. Cultural thought is conditioning people to seek freedom on their own terms and conditions, and certainly not those of SC. Those who thus consider themselves "free-thinkers" are not so much alluding to the foundations of the Enlightenment anymore, as they now really mean free from God and all His boring demands. Contextually, the Christian worldview is evaluated as repressive to how people should think, live their lives, and pursue whatever they desire. Surely one can "enjoy the passing pleasures of sin" (Heb. 11:25), but not without severe emotional consequences. So cultural thought now believes that once CF is removed then it's free to pursue whatever fulfillment it desires without any reminders of guilt from SC. Accordingly, subjectivism flourishes as everyone's interpretation of moral behaviour is free to decide its own threshold of right from wrong.

Quite naturally, in this environment the buzz word becomes, *tolerance*. Thus, SC clashes with cultural thought because SC is deemed intolerant towards the self-fulfilling pursuits prevalent in culture. Cultural thought likes a rigged game as one of its prized values is tolerance and it can tolerate quite a bit, but not when it comes to the values of SC. Culture promotes its sacred belief in tolerance and makes superficial gestures of tolerance towards CF. Note that in conversation, people in polite society now respond to a believer with superficiality: "I disagree with you, but if it makes you happy then that's okay *for you*." That is as far as culture goes in its tolerance of CF, and even those crumbs are beginning to be swept off of the table. At the core of this smoke-filled room, however, remains the human quest for individual happiness. People are increasingly depressed, lonely, and void of inner fulfillment.

When Jesus said, "I am the bread of life. He who comes to me shall never hunger, and he who believes in me shall never thirst" (Jn. 6: 35), He was revealing Himself as the God given satisfier of our inner most desire for fulfillment. Let us read His words again studiously, reflectively, and with serious intent: "*I am the bread of life.*" If this is true, without any exaggeration, then what on earth did Jesus intend for humankind? Could it really be available for us today as well? Indeed, it can. Scripture must be understood by what God intended for us, and not by what *we would like it to mean* for us today. So then, how did He intend for us to *understand and experience* this revelation? When Jesus says, "*I am*," is there any room for us to negotiate and apply an understanding of what cultural thought will sanction? Our human existence has always sought to satisfy itself, because to have a "life" is by definition to seek its fulfillment.

When Jesus said, "*I am the Bread of life*," He was revealing what God purposed for humanity's lasting fulfillment. It's a permanent, fixed, and indispensable revelation of our Creator's ongoing provision for our complete fulfillment in Jesus Christ. As Jesus confirmed, "He who comes to me shall *never* hunger, and he who believes in me shall *never* thirst." The more we taste and digest of this "Bread" the less our lives will be vulnerable to all of the other substitutes promoted within our culture. We will experience lives lived within our means and be very happy doing so. Believers must *know* what it means to experience this wonderful fulfillment by a deep relationship with Jesus.

Unless we do so, our CF will be frustrated by the creeping in of alternative substitutes which can never be a satisfactory replacement for "the Bread of Life." CF is intended to make us joyful, to provide an experience of real inner fulfillment, and to provide inner strength to serve and lead others effectively. Personal delight in CF can satisfy against the temptations of excess indulgence proffered incessantly on television, social media ads, internet banners, and even a casual walk in the mall. Eating the crumbs of this "Bread" will not satisfy the ongoing hunger in a culture replete with offers of fulfillment. Even weekly church attendance, or listening to an occasional sermon on podcasts, or reading intermittently about CF, or casually reading Scripture once in a while, are exercises that alone cannot compete with the constant appeals within culture. An ongoing experience of Jesus as "the Bread of Life" will nourish our CF and then there will be nothing else that could ever satisfy our inner being. We shall thus *"never hunger and never thirst."* We will then *know* how to live moderate and overwhelmingly fulfilled lives with our CF in culture.

Some are probably thinking: Sounds good, sounds like a noble ideal, but how is this even possible in our fast-paced lives? Such a question emerges from a premise that undervalues what SC is teaching us and overvalues what cultural thought is teaching. That is to say, we continue to emphasize biblical teaching, but the substance of SC is not communicated vigorously enough to shine its contrast on the culture's values of fulfillment. In addition, cultural thought emphasizes that we should embrace how technology has made our lives easier and much more fulfilling. Surely everyone appreciates how technology provides information, medical attention, ease of doing business, and instant communication, but we have been conditioned to be amazed at what we see, touch, and feel, and to place high value on such experiences. There is a real spiritual struggle within all believers today, a tug between our inner most longings to know God and the constant appeals of material things we experience daily. When CF is lived with these overwhelming distractions it becomes challenging to shift the mind's attention to comprehend fully what SC intends for believers. The occasional spark of Christian joy and peace is mistaken for a deep relationship with Jesus. It is in such sparks that many believers in North America have become stagnant. It's almost as if there is an embracing not of SC, but to its ideal. Depth of CF remains an ideal goal, but it's not being communicated enough as a realistic lifestyle to be appreciated and experienced. We thus need a refresher of what CF has accomplished in our lives and how its power has provided the "eternal" perspective on life in the here and now.

In any major city there is at least one main intersection where people are bustling. You should go there during rush hour, stand safely to the side, and watch the people. Then ask yourself, where are all these people going? Yes, they are going to work, to school, to do business, to shop, and to meetings. But where are they really going? What is their ultimate destination? There is a place which is now invisible, and sadly the salvation of their souls is the last thing on their minds. The minds are fastened on what Paul described as "temporal." You who are standing there will appreciate the "eternal" realities of life. Before your new birth you would have stood at that same intersection with your mind also on the "temporal." Now that you are "born of God" people appear different at this same intersection; their faces appear different; the clothes appear different; the window displays appear different; everything you see appears different, because the Spirit of God is in you. The Word of God has been confirmed in you: "... if anyone is in Christ, he is a new creation; old things have passed away; behold *all things have become new*" (2 Cor. 5:17).

You should balance your precious time in "the temporal," and explore these very real changes in your life. You will discover real fulfillment that will support you even during times of setbacks, which are inevitably part of the human experience in the "temporal." Others will be inspired by you and be blessed by the fruits of the Spirit demonstrated consistently through your character, "love, joy, peace, long-suffering, kindness, goodness, faithfulness, gentleness, self-control" (Gal. 5:22). You will seize the promise of Jesus: "I have come that they may have life, and that they may have it more abundantly" (Jn. 10:10). You will enter into a *real* deeper experience of CF. You will then have the strengths of joy and peace ruling your life, and influencing you to spend less time in the comfort zone. It's only when our CF is truly satisfying deep within that we will pursue servant leadership, meaningful community, healthier relationships, and whether we are high or low income earners our money will be placed happily into Kingdom perspective.

What will also make you see things differently within the crowd is "the light of life" within you. When light is turned on there is a clearer perspective on objects. The Word of God is described by the Psalmist as having the same effect: "Your word is a lamp to my feet and a light to my path" (Ps. 119:105). Without God's light humanity cannot see the beauty of how it was intended to live. When Isaiah prophesied of Christ he said, "There is no beauty that we should desire Him" (Is. 53:2). Jesus was a plain looking man without striking physical features. Yet more books have been written about Jesus than any other person in history. It was the beauty of His character, demeanor, personality, his use of illustrations to speak to humanity's heart and mind, and His display of the Spirit's power that drew people to Him. Jesus's life was marked by selflessness and yet His life impacted humankind more than anyone else. He remains the most mysterious person in history to those who do not know Him, but to His followers He provides "the light" from which Kingdom perspectives are breathtakingly beautiful.

With this "light" shining in our lives, we also cannot help but seek to demonstrate a beauty of character. "You are the light of the world," Jesus said, "A city that is set on a hill cannot be hidden" (Matt. 5:14). Something that is displayed with glaring visibility elicits attraction and wonder. When you visit a website, the opening window is carefully purposed to communicate something specific to you, and your interest should prompt you to wonder and be attracted to click further. Even department store windows are fashioned to draw maximum attention and interest. It's an ageless principle of humanity that something can be strategically placed to draw attention and wonder. Galleria Dell' Accademia in Florence strategically placed Michelangelo's "the David" at a spectacular space where it can impress on the viewer with maximum amazement and unending awe. "Let your light so shine before men," encouraged Jesus, "that they may see your good works and glorify your Father in heaven" (Matt. 5:16). The emphasis is on the "glory" of our "Father in heaven." When God gives us His "light" it is like a "lampstand" which "gives light to all who are in the house" (Matt. 5:15). In the previous chapter we also learned first-hand how various people from various cultures were all extraordinarily transformed by God's power of grace. These regenerated lives truly reflected "light" in the midst of "darkness."

Let's pause for a moment and reflect on our lives today in North America, from a supposedly scientific perspective. We read everywhere that life expectancy is around 80 for men and 84 for women. If you are 35, for example, and you live to the age of 84, then you have 588 months to go. I know, you can hardly believe that. If you are 50, you have 408 months left in your hour glass. Some of you are now calculating your numbers. Even as you are calculating, some of the grains of sand have already dropped to the bottom and continue to do so. Doesn't it put a different perspective on things? Activities should take on different priorities, shouldn't they? That comment I made earlier about our busyness being a myth now begins to make some sense, doesn't it? It now seems ludicrous to binge watch eight episodes of a program, doesn't it? "For what is your life?" James questions; "It is even a vapour that appears for a little time and then vanishes away" (4:14). Perhaps now we can appreciate more how Jesus cautioned "Martha" from fretting about all her distractions, and commended "Mary" for prioritizing "that good part."

Consistent with the teachings of SC Paul also called us to attention, "For we brought nothing into this world, and it is certain we can carry nothing out" (1 Tim. 6:7). Can you understand and appreciate your CF within the reality of your mortality? Is your CF acknowledging how high the stakes are in your relationship with Jesus? Was Amos joking around when he said, "Prepare to meet your God" (4:12)? Or perhaps he was genuinely mistaken? Could it be that we are not really convinced of what Amos said? Humanity cannot escape this ultimate encounter with its Creator, and as Christians we have the Good News. Thus, the clash with cultural thought as the human experience finds God irresistibly compelling, but definitely cannot bear to hear our message which is deemed judgmental, narrow-minded, restrictive, and anachronistic. Our personal experience of *knowingness* should continue to persuade us otherwise and challenge us to provide meaningful articulations to a culture steeped in Scriptural indifference.

With a real experience of CF in spite of cultural thought, believers should apply themselves to explore the purpose of it all in this age. The overwhelming reality of our mortality should also engender a deeper curiosity as to what SC means to us and then seek to communicate it intelligently with all of its power. Note that the missional values of a successful corporation are meant to create a cultural realization of their purpose and goals. How much more should we seek to know what the purposes and goals of SC are for humankind, and then by the Spirit influence one person at a time?

Perhaps one of the greatest moments in the Bible was when God asked Adam, "Where are you" (Gen. 3:9)? Surely God knew. He was looking for Adam like the Shepherd searching for His lost sheep. God's intended relationship with Adam remained a priority. People are the intended purpose and goal of SC. Our neighbours, friends, and colleagues are all the object of His love and grace. Even when we mess up, He seeks to reconcile us. God remains patiently reasonable with us: "Come now, and let us reason together, says the Lord, though your sins are like scarlet, they shall be as white as snow" (Is. 1:18). Adam and Eve received plenty from God, and when they demonstrated rebellion by disobeying one basic commandment God immediately set out on repairing the broken relationship.

So then, if the grace of God makes sense then why aren't more people converting? The main impasse to CF is not one's need for evidence. Cultural thought would like people to believe that it is and thereby reducing CF to a mere preference or to something that fulfills a personal crutch. The impasse, rather, is a reticent belief within cultural thought that the fun stuff will have to be abandoned in favour of a lifestyle of reciting prayers, lighting candles, and following a bunch of boring rules which stifle human progress. That is what the unregenerate mind in culture thinks of CF, whereas it is neither of those things. Nevertheless, that is indeed the primary misconception which remains latent in culture. CF is almost always mistaken as a conversion to a lifestyle of religious rituals, and hardly ever as a personal relationship with Jesus. Remember that looking through the glass "Door" of a restaurant is not the same as walking through it and enjoying the dining experience. Our mission is to emphasize that grace does make sense, and restoration to God is not a conversion to a strict lifestyle of observances but a personal relationship with Jesus. The Spirit will take care of the rest.

Cultural thought has dampened the purposed significance of SC and undermined it as "culturally regressive." Tim Keller experiences this first hand in his own NYC church. He writes,

The Christian faith requires belief in the Bible. This is a big stumbling block for many. I meet many New Yorkers for the first time after they have been invited to one of Redeemer's services. The centerpiece of each service is a sermon based on a text of the Bible. The average visitor is surprised or even shocked to find us listening to the Bible so carefully. Most would say that they know there are many great stories and sayings in the Bible, but today 'you can't take it *literally*.' What they mean is that the Bible is not entirely trustworthy because some parts - maybe many or most parts - are scientifically impossible, historically unreliable, and culturally regressive.[47] Our audience now considers itself sophisticatedly beyond belief in SC, with reluctance towards faith values. All over North America a new generation of Christian leaders are desperately trying to respond to the culture's criticisms of CF. I believe that what is emerging is an approach that is sensitive to cultural thought and careful not to offend the "intelligence" of the unchurched. Increasingly, our church sanctuaries are catering to what are believed to be the underlying expectations of those who walk through our doors.

The church experience seeks to be free from any of the negative stereotypes perceived by culture. Some Christian leaders have cleverly dissected cultural thought and have decided to avoid using the terms that will turn people off, such as, repentance, sin, holiness, and eternal damnation. They have rightly perceived that cultural thought is sympathetic to Jesus, but it dislikes Christians and churches. We here it often, "I like Jesus; it's the Christians and the churches who are hypocritical." Cultural thought has surely thrown some cold water in the face of contemporary Christianity. For their efforts and zeal, contemporary Christian leaders should be commended for applying themselves to reach cultured people, but we should not allow cultural thought to intimidate us into watering down SC. The ministerial task is to provide counter

---

[47] Tim Keller, *The Reason for God: Belief in an Age of Skepticism* (New York: Penguin Group, 2008), 99-100.

culturally nuanced communications that demonstrate a knowledge of contemporary times and a faithfulness to SC.

One thing remains certain: People continue to hunger for real SC. Innovations that try to eliminate the perceptions of a judgmental attitude in our faith communities are commendable, but people are drawn to attend Christian meetings by an expectation of substance. Recently, *Christianity Today* reported that,

Despite a new wave of contemporary church buzzwords like relational, relevant, and intentional, people who show up on Sundays are looking for the same thing that has long anchored most services: preaching centered on the Bible. 'Sermons that teach about Scripture' are the No. 1 reason Americans go to church, according to a new Gallup poll. . .. Preaching on Scripture and its relevance ranked above factors like kids' programs, . . . community outreach, . . . and social activities. . . Even so-called seeker sensitive churches have discovered that theological depth appeals to lapsed Christians and non-believers. . .. 'In other words, those for whom sermons were being dumbed down aren't dumb. They are interested in the truth or else they'd be out golfing.'[48]

What is also revealing about this research is "that people in the pews care far more about what's being preached then who is

---

[48] Kate Shellnutt, "The Hottest Thing at Church Is Not Your Pastor or Worship Leader," *Christianity Today* (April 18, 2017): Online, *https://www.christianitytoday.com/news/2017/april/gallup-hottest-thing-at-church-not-pastor-worship.html*. Although this was an American report, I believe there are parallels for Canadians.

preaching it."[49] Peoples' hunger for SC transcends the celebrity status draw of preachers who are highlighted in our North American church model. If this is so, then anyone communicating SC in a Christian meeting should diligently seek to connect effectively with people. One's communication of SC in any setting, one on one, small groups, or from the platform on Sunday mornings, must demonstrate a personal sense of *knowingness* about SC. Do you think that a listener would be captivated by a communicator who has clearly not experienced the deep convictions of SC? You cannot communicate something that you do not have.

With great emotion Jesus said, "He who has ears to hear, let him hear" (Luke 8:8). Everyone "has ears to hear" so the point of Jesus is that everyone should take heed! People do give us opportunities to communicate our CF, but will they listen with "ears to hear." A combination of knowledge, passion, experience, and personal persuasion must be reflected in our communication. Avoiding unpopular words such as, sin, repentance, and holiness should not be out of fear that we will be deemed unsophisticated or uncool. When such terms are communicated with cultural intelligence and personal conviction of SC people will want to know more. Gospel communicators must become what Matthew D. Kim describes as "bridge builders." He writes:

> What knowledge do we currently possess about various listeners as we prepare to preach to them? For instance, what beliefs or values influence their daily decisions? . . . On what

---

[49] Ibid.

do they spend their time and resources? What types of food do your listeners eat, and what do they decline? What cultural values are most highly esteemed in their culture: honesty, hard work, success, age, education, profession, salary, position, status? What cultural idols obstruct the gospel from taking root in their lives, and more?[50]

I believe people will find our answers to these questions compellingly striking when we weave an intelligent connection with them and demonstrate the relevancy of SC.

When Jesus began His ministry the first word He uttered was "*Repent*." When he began to send His disciples "two by two . . . they went out and preached that people should *repent*" (Mar. 6:12). In Acts, after a sermon from Peter, the listeners said with great conviction "to Peter and the rest of the apostles, 'Men and brethren, what shall we do?' Then Peter and the rest of the apostles said to them, '*Repent*, and let every one of you be baptized in the name of Jesus Christ for the remission of sins'" (Acts 2:37-38). Later Peter preached another sermon and concluded with, "*Repent* therefore . . ." (Acts 3:19). When Paul preached his memorable sermon to the Athenians he concluded with "God . . . now commands all men everywhere to *repent*" (Acts 17:29). Even so, the Pauline Epistles developed a theology on repentance, grace, and justifying faith. This is SC. I admit that it's not easy to communicate a straightforward call to repentance in contemporary culture. Of

---

[50] Matthew D. Kim, *Preaching with Cultural Intelligence: Understanding the People Who Hear Our Sermons* (Grand Rapids: Baker Academic, 2017), 7.

course, Christian leaders should be sensitive to the unchurched with the realization that today's seeker is quite sophisticated. We should not, however, be duped into thinking that a call to repentance will turn people off, while making ourselves appear as unsophisticated, regressive and irrelevant thinkers. A fresh and thoughtful communication of what the depths of SC were purposed to accomplish in people's lives is desperately required, without reluctance that it will be deemed regressive.

Again, contemporary Christian leaders should be commended for discerning cultural thought and working diligently to make the Gospel relevant. The new measures of doing church are not altogether feckless. It's the content of the message that requires robust encouragement. As the article in *CT* noted, people do not want to hear a "dumb downed" presentation of Scripture. If you have been a Christian for a while you can attend any church, Bible study, life group, or prayer meeting, and the content will be predictable. Going forward, much discipline will be required in order to rise up and learn how to articulate Scriptural repentance, with keen sensitivity, with careful exposition, and with communication that addresses how people are being influenced to think by culture. We can no longer assume that our listeners will simply accept an unpacking of a Scriptural passage.

People are now influenced by a cultural thought that has its own fabricated meaning of God, that is, of denying and re-imagining Him apart from SC in order to accommodate our unrelenting need for Him. About a decade ago this thinking was highlighted in *Reinventing the Sacred*. The author attempted to reconstruct an *idea* of God which contemporary people can use for individual meaning in a progressive world. He wrote,

No, we do not have to use the *God* word, but it may be wise to do so to help orient our lives. This sense of God enlarges Western humanism for those who do not believe in a Creator God. It invites those who hold to a supernatural Creator God to sustain that faith, but to allow the creativity in the universe to be a further source of meaning and membership.[51]

Humanity is progressing, but it hasn't abandoned its attempt to reconcile with its indistinguishable sense of God. Our listeners are encountering such ideas in literature, film, television programs, and everywhere online, but their inner need for God remains. That is why many are looking for a message that communicates substance on how CF can apply to their everyday secular experiences.

With no connection there is no meaningful impact, and with no impact there is no real benefit gained by a hearing of SC. When SC is communicated the Spirit should cause a real connection with our listeners. People should be made to consider keenly what is presented. Even if they disagree with us, they should nevertheless be impressed enough to consider Scriptural claims, and to realize that it's different from pre-conceived stereotypes within culture. Our goal should not be to hear that our presentation was

---

[51] Stuart A. Kauffman, *Reinventing the Sacred: A New Vision of Science, Reason, and Religion* (New York: Perseus Books Group, 2010), 285. I see this as an attempt to reconcile the reality of humanity's ongoing inner convictions of God. The book is a "reinvention" of God to fit into one's commitments to secular thinking. People need the substance of SC even in a rapidly progressing culture, because the human constitution will never be complete without the grace of God.

wonderful or that it was funny, though humour is sometimes appropriate, but how it made them think and how their hearts were moved unlike anything they have heard. The Word hasn't changed. We must learn to apply the timeless Word to people who have undergone a cultural shift by the influence of secular ideas about God. A communication of CF must acknowledge how the listeners are being influenced by culture and then present accordingly.

We have all heard a message which really connected with us and made SC a beautiful experience. What was different? Clearly, the presenter had really thought through SC and from a deep personal experience of it, and insights of contemporary culture, connected by making us understand and experience the beauty of CF in our context. We have all heard, read, or viewed something that makes the light go on in our minds, like an "aha" moment. The Spirit of God is all about making connections with people. Next time you talk about SC, whether one on one, or to a small or large group, seriously ask yourself this: How is cultural thought affecting my listeners? What is it that I am trying to accomplish? What is the point of my communication to the listener? What will be the great takeaway? Jesus and the Apostles knew what they wanted for their audiences. Do you know what you want for yours?

The Apostles Peter and John were uneducated fisherman when they were initially called by Jesus. When they had finished communicating SC to a group of educated religious leaders it says in Acts: "Now when they saw the boldness of Peter and John, and perceived that they were uneducated and untrained men, they marveled. And they realized that they had been with Jesus" (4:13). Our persuasion of the truth of SC will only come when we have "been with Jesus." Jesus knew that only His power could provide spiritual victory for His followers. When His power is in us, we will know it and others will too. Have you ever heard a presentation of SC in the manner of Paul who said, "And my speech and my preaching were not with persuasive words of human wisdom, but in demonstration of the Spirit and of power, that your faith should not be in the wisdom of men but in the power of God" (1 Cor. 2:4-5)? Such communications will only come from those who have disciplined themselves in the school of Jesus, which is for all His followers. Note that when Jesus commended Martha's sister Mary, He intended the lesson on priorities for everyone in the room.

From deep within, we must treasure our Gospel message and treat it as something extremely precious. Our message of SC has become way too ordinary. We have heard about God loving the world and sending His Son so many times that its pristine intentions have faded. We need to refresh our appreciation of the Gospel. Think about it. CF has the power to provide emotional healing and forgiveness for people without it costing them anything, and without any conditions. We are in possession of a message in SC that can provide immeasurable inner fulfillment, joy, peace, and new found love for all people. Are you kidding me? Seriously? If this is all true then let us rise up and think of how we should begin to treat this message and how to communicate it to a culture that has blinded itself into Scriptural indifference. There should be no way that such a powerful message should receive yawns from cultural thought. We must begin to apply ourselves faithfully, intellectually, with love and wisdom, with the keen insights of SC, and seek to communicate cogently in all of our fields, industries, and every other engagement with culture.

In North America, our God given resources are immense. We have countless seminaries, universities and schools, institutes, think tanks, churches and fellowships, gifted pastors and teachers, evangelists, youth leaders, the wisdom of Elder boards, para church ministries, apologists, professors, scholars, writers, bloggers, artists, musicians, filmmakers, mentors, coaches, scientists, philosophers, psychologists and psychiatrists, physicians, powerful and gifted business people, lawyers, politicians, voices on the radio, on television, on social media, and even movie stars and celebrities. How is it, then, that our CF is allowing secularism to dominate cultural thought and reinterpret our own beliefs? How is it that church attendance is declining? How is it also that young people are increasingly losing interest in SC? Somewhere, somehow, something has gone drastically wrong with our endeavours.

Perhaps the material comforts have simply gotten the better of us and sedated our CF? Or perhaps all of our resources are identifying with Martha and have neglected to keep their CF consistently fresh by "the one thing needed"? With all of our resources, if every believer began to exercise a bit of discipline in their relationship with Jesus, we should surely have a serious impact in culture. Our contemporary situation is not insurmountable. It is truly an exciting opportunity for us to collaborate with one another's gifts and talents, with the intention of understanding our cultural milieu and deploying our resources intelligently. We can introduce many to the wonderful redemptive power of Jesus. The Gospel is so powerful that if every believer truly appreciated it and committed their time, gifts, talents, and resources, with disciplined lifestyles, our churches and fellowships would be flourishing.

Sure, it will take time, years, even a lifetime. Each believer must begin to thirst for a deeper experience of SC. As Jesus "cried out" in the midst of a crowd, "if anyone thirsts, let him come to me and drink. He who believes in me, as the Scripture has said, out of his heart will flow rivers of living water" (Jn. 7:37-38). This promise is not reserved for a select few whose theological curiosity seeks satisfaction, but intended for every believer. When you drink of His water the inner fulfillment will radiate from you. Distractions and material comforts will occupy less space in your life, because they cannot compete with the "rivers of living water." With God's presence in our lives it's not too late to exercise the discipline required to discover "the unsearchable riches of Christ" (Eph. 3:8). Best of all, God promises: "I will certainly be with you" (Ex. 3:12). God's presence in our lives can become an unmistakable experience, and teach us why He commanded first: "You shall have no other gods before me" (Ex. 20:3).

Perhaps you are a bit apprehensive about the challenge to deepen your relationship with Jesus, not really knowing what will happen. Or perhaps your concern might be that allowing more space to learn about Jesus will cause you to miss out on all the fun stuff. Really? Or maybe your hesitation is simply that you don't want to get too much into SC. After all, moderation is another important buzz word in cultural thought. Maybe we cannot realistically afford the time to do what the Psalmist said, "Evening and morning and at noon I will pray, and cry aloud, and He shall hear my voice" (Ps. 55:17). That is truly understandable. Nurturing a family, earning a living, getting an education, or building a relationship, are necessary pursuits that require time. As Christians, however, we cannot afford to neglect some Jesus time as we pursue our normal course of life. You will be utterly amazed at how even a brief time every day at the feet of Jesus, like Mary, seeking "that good part," studying and learning about Him, will impact all areas of your life. Accept the challenge, prioritize Jesus and squeeze a bit of time for Him every day, and in short order joy and peace will increase; you will be wiser; your career will be more rewarding and fulfilling; your productivity will rise; your faith community life will be more meaningful. Your family, friends, and colleagues will notice your character transformation. Your relationship with Jesus will reveal itself to you as the most valuable thing imaginable.

We should also acknowledge that we are living in an era where the self is craving insatiable attention. We have capabilities now to draw instant attention to ourselves and it has become intoxicating. Social media are also influencing behaviours that a generation ago were unimaginable. Or perhaps online platforms are magically producing new characters out of people? Regardless, online platforms have taken on a competitive nature that not only drives believers to distinguish themselves and compete for attention, but they even provide concrete measurements in order to gauge our popularity. Everyone can now scientifically measure their popularity. Christ followers are living in a very complicated culture.

Chapter 3

GOD'S GIFTS IN AN ERA OF SELFIES

"He must increase, but I must decrease" John 3:30

We have heard the saying that a picture is worth a thousand words; but in this era, it has been narrowed down to three, *me, myself and I*. People post pictures online constantly of their achievements, celebrations, personal milestones, moments of apparent happiness, and most of all snapshots of self. More than any previous era people today love to display pictures of themselves. Others may politely tolerate one's snapshots of success, but they are far more interested and passionate about posting their own pictures for others to admire. Narcissistic temptations are pushing many on social media to crave for the attention which is abundantly supplied. Social media ignite the competitive spirit in most people, believers too. I recall a Christian lady who posted her son's first term university report card and it was impressive, straight As. Such a posting is clearly indicative of how people cannot resist the temptation to aggrandize themselves before a captive audience.

Some of you might disagree, believing that if people have a problem with that posting then it's their problem. Note, however, that most compliments such postings receive are not as genuine as you might think. The next time you receive a compliment on how great your kid is, take it with a grain of salt, because almost all such commentators prefer to see the promotion of their kids, and I think you do too. There is a competitiveness to social media and this is why believers should learn how to communicate their offline giftedness to their online presence. Make no mistake about it: The human connections on social media can become real and our God given gifts can potentially influence others.

What I said in the previous chapter about material things not going away, and not intrinsically bad, I also say about social media. Online platforms are providing an extraordinary opportunity for our gifts to shine and to influence people with the Gospel in ways unimaginable to previous generations of Christ ambassadors. Given that social media is only going to get more sophisticated by web analytics, how then do we apply our God given gifts to our online presence and "increase Him"? It will thus "be interesting to reflect on the ways that the online environment provides opportunities for people to present themselves . . . in the image of a loving and relational God whose abundant gifts to us define our identity." [52] Technology, however, will continue to tempt the Christian witness to increase self and to build individual attention grabbing communications. It is all so exhilarating to see yourself portrayed and garnering attention, while also looking secretly at what others are doing and then plotting for an edge to compete. Nevertheless, the opportunity to communicate our CF online in ways that demonstrate a powerful connection of grace and truth with people is unprecedented.

---

[52] Lynne M. Baab, "Toward a Theology of the Internet: Place, Relationship, and Sin," In *Digital Religion, Social Media and Culture*, eds. Pauline Hope Cheong, Peter Fischer-Nielsen, Stefan Gelgren, Charles Ess (New York: Peter Lang, 2012), 277-292.

CF is an emotionally charged topic online, as trolling is common and sometimes nasty. People react because the demands of SC can convict, challenge, and compel people even through social media platforms. Even online the Word of God can be "living and powerful, and sharper than any two-edged sword, piercing . . . the division of soul and spirit" (Heb. 4:12). When our giftedness is translated online with passionate focus and humble determination it can have far reaching influence. An international conversation is happening on Social Media and SC is becoming part of it and hopefully the beauties of its message will shine. At the onset of social media Christians began with some highly influential movement, even drawing the curiosity of mainstream culture. As Tim Challies noted,

> Hundreds of thousands of Christian blogs sprang up, influencing the church in powerful ways. One of *Time* magazine's '10 Ideas Changing the World Right Now in 2009' was New Calvinism. . . It is a movement that relied heavily on Christian blogs and social media, one that would not have happened without them.[53]

You see how we have the potential to create influence online with our gifts, gaining the attention of *Time* and its readers?

What is important to note is that even though cultural thought is generally antagonistic to CF many secular people may still consider spiritual matters when they are alone. One enthusiast for

---

[53] Tim Challies, *The Next Story: Life After the Digital Explosion* (Grand Rapids: Zondervan, 2011), 71.

communicating the Gospel online commented with insight that, "People do their secret thinking on the internet, and because of that people explore things on the web - such as who Jesus Christ is - that they can't or won't explore in public."[54] Opportunities to show the Gospel's relevancy can potentially translate online to impact people everywhere. We should begin by dispelling the myth that most unbelievers online are not interested, are not redeemable, and so let's communicate among ourselves. Let us acknowledge, rather, that all people have feelings, emotions, shortcomings, and experience sin. The "redeemed" should become confidant in communicating SC online, with love, kindness, and engaging articulations that will connect with people.

Huge banners, slogans, or even quoting Scripture alone without a brief and thoughtful commentary, will not always connect with everyone. Such can provide encouragement to those who are already in the fold, but they often do little for those whose minds have been tainted by the stereotypes of CF prevalent in culture. Thoughtful explanations and well-articulated communications will pique interest, even if people are not showing any likes. A careful and savvy communication of the Gospel can be a huge influence on social media, for people are doing "their secret thinking" online. Accordingly, Twitter has become ideal for what Jesus taught in the parable of the sower: "Behold, a sower went out to sow. And he sowed, some . . . fell on good ground and yielded a crop" (Matt. 13:4-8). We have unprecedented

---

[54] Bryony Taylor, "Sharing Faith Using Social Media," *Grove Evangelism* (EV 115, 2016): 1-28.

opportunities online to sow seeds of CF. The Jesus approach of continually engaging people with the power of Truth can be part of our online conversation. Unfortunately, believers are being swept up in the illusion of social media, and merely sprinkling on some faith talk.

The focus on me, myself, and I, truly augmented itself in public consciousness with the onset of the selfie stick, the reverse camera feature on our phones, and instant access to social media apps where excessive self-expression constantly tempts everyone. As for Christians, the virtues of SC are being challenged unlike any other time and the communication of one's God given gifts and talents require some recalibration.[55] In Romans 11:29 we read that, "the gifts and the calling of God are irrevocable." That is to say, gifts are without God's regret even in this age of social media platforms. Using God's gifts and talents online are not the problem at all, even though the appetite to show oneself off influences how believers do ministry on social media. Gifts are now measured by how many impressions, views, likes, friends, followers, and retweets one will receive if they massage their presentation in a certain way, and this quest for numerical recognition has indeed influenced communication. As one Christian blogger explained, "Even when it comes to writing this blog, when I concentrate on writing the

---

[55] In addition to the specific "spiritual gifts" described in Scripture I will also use the term "gifts" to mean our natural gifts and talents which God has bestowed to believers. All of these "gifts" are used by the Spirit for "the work of ministry" and to contribute to the enrichment of everyone's CF.

best, most helpful content for readers, I write one way. But when I'm trying to get the number of page views up, I write differently."[56]

Once upon a time, photo booths were used with curtains drawn and portraits were not meant to garner public attention. Pictures were kept mostly for private use. Even photos of family and friends on vacation or celebrating milestones were placed in an album for selective showings. Anyone who would have developed the photos and posted them somewhere public for everyone to see would have been deemed peculiar or even daft. Showing one's snapshots publicly was not part of the culture, and so the temptation to seek attention was not widespread. Today, social media platforms provide opportunity for everyone to share their lives online and it's all normal. The temptation for everyone is to seek admiration from followers by displaying how great their lives appear. This online context is that of Christians too, where we also represent our CF. Our communications of SC will either seek to connect with people or be caught up in the frenzy of seeking attention and building up a following to validate our

---

[56] Karl Vaters, "Caring Or Counting? The Pastoral Dilemma," *Christianity Today* (January 22, 2019): Online, *https://www.christianitytoday.com/karl-vaters/2019/january/caring-or-counting-pastoral-dilemma.html.* Note that I have cited Vaters to emphasize my point that online attention can influence how we communicate our CF. Nevertheless, Vaters does also note in the article: "To be clear, I've only written that way a handful of times. It's never been mean spirited, and it's never caused me to write anything theologically compromised. Also, I haven't written one like that in several years...."

supposed influence. We are all gifted by God and so we can either increase the presence of Jesus reflectively or we can exercise our gifts egoistically.

Culturally, selfies have come to convey that I matter too, that I can also be cool, successful, accomplished, and that I am also experiencing something that everyone else should take note of. Look at me, I am seated near the players at a major sports event because I am doing something right and this picture proves it. Every follower is now compelled to admire me and take note of my success. Selfies have provided an opportunity for us to accentuate ourselves deliberately, and to do so easily and rapidly. It is all so enchanting. Competition to distinguish oneself has even influenced businesses to supply for the demand. Marketers are capitalizing on this selfie culture as their primary goal now is to convince you that their product will make you feel and look as great as possible for everyone else to admire. Even so, there are now locations popping up all over North America where you pay an entrance fee to access exhibits of illusion. Inside there are various rooms where illusory backdrops provide for snapping selfies that will distinguish you with great effect. Persons can then instantly show them off to others. Instantly! To the whole world! Even churches are beginning to provide space for backdrops in order to facilitate selfies.[57]

---

[57] Kate Shellnutt, "Welcome to Church, Want to Take a Selfie?" *Christianity Today* (May 13, 2019): Online, *https://www.christianitytoday.com/ct/2019/may-web-only/church-photo-booth-backdrops-instagram-mothers-day.html.*

Of course, self-portraits have long been part of a human desire to express itself. Now that technology is in everyone's hands, "We no longer need to rely on others to represent us. We represent ourselves."[58] We can also do so quite easily, economically, and with fantastic outreach. Thereby the opportunity to make oneself the object of instant adoration becomes irresistible; and in this context, believers are challenged to communicate their gifts and point people to SC. Whether it is blogging, or a presentation on YouTube, or sharing resources for effective ministry on our online platforms, almost everyone is being tempted by an obsession with attention to self.

Going forward, we should explore how our gifts can become valuable and altruistic in their intentions to communicate SC online. Our communications should rise above a strict fixation on numerical achievement, and be more concerned with the "resonance factor." It is a monumental challenge, but it should become foremost on our social media platforms. I like how Leonard Sweet put it in *Viral*:

> For followers of Jesus, the power of influence should never have been based on rank but on resonance. . .. When something resonates, we hear words of the same substance that is found in our souls. When something resonates, we find that others are like us when we were convinced we were alone in

[58] Jill Walker Rettberg, *Seeing Ourselves Through Technology: How We Use Selfies, Blogs, and Wearable Devices to See and Shape Ourselves* (New York: Palgrave Macmillan, 2014), 88.

feeling this. When something resonates, we feel the vibration in our souls.[59]

With God's gifts, knowing how to make others "feel the vibration in our souls" is what social media ministry must do in order to make SC *resonant*. Can you imagine if every God given gift were used to make communications of SC on social media resonate? When God's gifts are used egoistically, and it's quite easy in a culture of selfies, believers are tempted to climb in "rank" for maximum recognition rather than concentrating on how best to make their CF resonate. We must appreciate the fact that our giftedness now has the potential for a phenomenal outreach to everyone's indispensable personal device.

As a Christian with such capability, the challenge to glorify Jesus and bless others before ourselves is enormous, especially in a culture where it is now counter intuitive to place others before oneself. If I were to ask you who is the greatest Biblical character, you would probably answer, Moses, Abraham, or the Apostle Paul. They are not. Neither is Ruth, Esther, King Solomon, Peter, John the beloved disciple of Jesus, nor Mary, or Joseph. "For I say to you," said Jesus authoritatively, "among those born of women there is not a greater prophet than John the Baptist" (Luke 7:28). Of all the prophets he had the greatest gift, and when Jesus appeared John immediately directed everyone's attention to Him. John's gift remained faithful to God and translated to what it was given to do. The Scriptures teach us that, "John saw Jesus coming

---

[59] Leonard Sweet, *Viral: How Social Networking Is poised to Ignite Revival* (Colorado Springs: WaterBrook Press, 2012), 81.

toward him, and said, 'Behold! The Lamb of God who takes away the sin of the world!" (Jn. 1:29). As we are now part of an unstoppable social network will we learn from the greatest prophet of all time and point people to Jesus with our gifts? Or will we use God's gifts to point attention to ourselves? As pointed out in *Click2Save*, "Generally speaking, a strong social media presence that best articulates a clear and distinctive voice . . . is not self-promoting."[60] From within, we must identify with what John the Baptist said, "He must increase, but I must decrease." Then we will begin to understand how God's gifts can influence people effectively online.

Unfortunately, the Scriptural way of giftedness is not promoted or emphasized enough in our fellowships. First, *all* believers should know that they are gifted by God for one or more areas of ministry, and their offline giftedness can be translated to communicate effectively online. With such a dearth of teaching, fellowships rely on the promotion of God's gifts according to natural standards. Attention is thus directed at individuals with worldly success rather than identifying the Spirit's gifts to all believers and encouraging their development. We are now conditioned to believe that naturally talented people who are successful outside of our fellowship can transition their talents into the fellowship, but this criterion requires a fresh understanding of SC. Our ministry mentality on giftedness must now broaden as our online presence inevitably expands with a cacophony of voices. If

---

[60] Elizabeth Drescher, Keith Anderson, *Click2Save: The Digital Ministry Bible* (New York: Morehouse Publishing, 2012), 42.

we are to acknowledge the supremacy of our Lord Jesus and share our deepening relationship with Him, Christian leaders must begin to acknowledge, affirm, develop, and promote all of God's genuine gifts both offline and for online potential.

Should we continue on without recognizing and promoting the gifts God has placed among us then authentic and mature CF will be difficult to communicate online, because if everyone is aimlessly clamoring for attention then the few distinct voices will be muffled. God's gifts must occupy their places so that the Spirit can accomplish His desires in our bodily community and on our social media platforms. I am persuaded that the two must become equally developed if we are to touch people with the Gospel in an emerging culture of social media. Growing fellowships should identify gifts and provide education on how to translate a relationship with Jesus online, for they can have enormous influence. Giftedness among us and how we prepare for ministry is changing quickly.

A paradigm shift may be occurring in the traditional method of acknowledging God's gifts and how believers are commissioned with an endorsement to proclaim the Gospel. Let me now highlight some of the traditional ways which are being challenged by an emerging generation of gifted online communicators. We have a structure in North America whereby denominations affirm gifted leadership based on specific and rigorous processes. Christians are required to attend the seminary of their denomination for training and then begin the processes of having their gifts validated for ministry. The candidates are appointed to work with seasoned mentors who monitor and provide opportunities to teach and preach with the goal of ordination or a professorship.

In a distinguished seminary associated with a big denomination, one's gifts have greater potential for validation and marketability. I remember my first term at an evangelical graduate school in the USA, and settling in the dormitory. A few days later another student arrived in his early twenties, and in the course of our introductory conversation he mentioned how delighted he was to have been accepted, and that upon hearing of his acceptance his denomination had already offered him a noteworthy position. Even before graduating! Upon acceptance, he began the process of being groomed with the authority to represent his denomination and become an authorized voice, eventually with letters and titles before and after his name. This thinking has been embedded in how we develop God's giftedness, but it appears at risk of being replaced. Online capabilities should now be alerting us that many who may appear as unlikely candidates through the lens of our traditional structures now have a voice. Distinguished degrees and titles will continue to have a place in training pastors and teachers, but social media platforms are providing "authority" to many believers who do not fit the traditional understanding of God's giftedness and now have the capability to minister and organize gatherings. All believers can start a YouTube channel. If they have God's giftedness to communicate CF, they will find a following.

Let's say, for example, that in a fellowship of 500 adherents, a devoted, gifted, and articulate young Christian lady has 450 followers on her social media platform with whom she engages often to teach SC. Who are now the gifted influencers in this fellowship? The pastoral staff? The elder board? No, they are no longer the only ones whose gifts are influential. She now has influence with her gifts. The traditional means of developing and affirming God's gifts among us are being challenged. Education and denominational processes will continue to facilitate God's gifts and will be used by Him to enrich our fellowships, but they are being challenged as the sole qualifier for gifted ministry. Could it be, then, that going forward in this culture of self-centeredness that if we are not vigilant in our teaching and developing of God's gifts, we could potentially allow artificial gifts to influence us online without realizing it?

Cultural thought is now moving towards acknowledging an "authority" by one's social media status. The temptation for any Christian seeking to be an authority now hinges on numerical achievement on social media. The understanding of authority is shifting from the traditional tracks of education, training, and relevant experience to popularity online. Note the analyses in *Networked Theology*:

> . . . in new-media culture authority may be constituted primarily on the basis of reputation systems (i.e., number of likes on Facebook, followers on Twitter, link rankings on blogs). It is the breath of one's social network online that elevates one's voice and position online. This means that who is the legitimate voice for a particular community is changing in the internet age."[61]

---

[61] Heidi A. Campbell, Stephen Garner, *Network Theology: Negotiating Faith in Digital Culture* (Grand Rapids: Baker Academics, 2016), 75.

Our fellowships ought to implement gifted social platform facilitators who can recognize God's gifts among us and seriously plan to develop them, especially as we continue to increase our online presence. We cannot constrain ourselves to developing only those who satisfy the traditional expectations for ministry. New "authorities" are emerging, and the reality is that *we can't stop what is happening*. What we can do is increase training and awareness of how to communicate our offline experiences of CF to an online community. As a believer's giftedness extends its reach, we should hope its "voice" will communicate the substance of SC in a manner that resonates. Otherwise, what is the point of using one's giftedness to attract an audience to oneself, and not to the real grace and truths of God?

Growing communities of faith should thus seek to educate on the right motives with an online use of God's gifts, because it is becoming irresistibly tempting to promote what culture wishes to hear online at the expense of genuine SC. Paul did say, "For the time will come when they will not endure sound doctrine, but according to their own desires . . . they will heap up for themselves teachers; and they will turn their ears away from the truth, and be turned aside to fables" (2 Tim. 4: 3-4). As I already remarked, SC will never be considered "cool" by cultural thought and so it behooves us more than ever to articulate SC effectively online. All ministries are now extremely sensitive to what the responses will be to their writings, sermons, worship, and any Scriptural interpretations posted online. The temptation to dilute SC in order to gain cultural favour is affecting all believers at every level of ministry.

It is also affecting every Christian blogger and communicator on social media to hanker for popularity, because this is gradually becoming the benchmark by how God's giftedness is affirmed. Many are discovering how unpopular one can become if CF were communicated in a certain way, and how popular if communicated in another way. Can you see how the depths of SC can become non-influential in this culture, with more focus on what will drive popularity even at the expense of diluting SC? Many are being influenced to increase self while the Lord Himself is decreasing.

The internet has made it possible for anyone to make it into public consciousness where an exaggerated sense of one's self-importance is projected. One's online presence could increase dramatically and then interest in that person rises, with the belief that their material must be better than the others because of its popularity. If a spiritually gifted believer evidently attracts an enormous amount of online attention then the artificial belief is that other believers should likewise compete to validate their own gift. I am not suggesting that those who lead megachurches or those whose individual ministries have gained enormous attention are either wrongly motivated or not gifted by God. Not at all. What I am highlighting is that our validations of God's gifts among us are now at risk of being assessed not by how they will promote CF and edify believers, but by how the gifts can assist one's ministry to achieve enormous popularity. This is becoming an irresistible (and intoxicating) pursuit.

Scripturally speaking, however, God's gifts are not given so that individuals can promote themselves, but that all believers are "equipped" to serve and together achieve "the stature of the fullness of Christ" even with social media. In Ephesians, Paul writes:

But to each one of us grace was given according to the measure of Christ's gift. . . . And He Himself gave some to be apostles, some prophets, some evangelists, and some pastors and teachers, for the equipping of the saints for the work of ministry, for the edifying of the body of Christ, till we all come to the unity of the faith and of the knowledge of the Son of God, to a perfect man, to the measure of the stature of the fullness of Christ (4:7-13).

My purpose here is not to discuss whether or not apostolic or prophetic succession is active today. As for evangelists, they are gifted with proclaiming the Good News and some could even do so with their online presence. As well, missionaries could very well be considered as gifted evangelists who are sent out to proclaim the Gospel in remote places. They have a gift for persuading and bringing people to reconcile with God, and this gift can also be developed to minister online. Unfortunately, we have come to perceive the gifted evangelist solely as one who is head and shoulders above everyone else in charisma and whose special ministry conducts crusades internationally. There may continue to be a place for such ministry. However, there are many gifted evangelists among us who should be affirmed and given resources to exercise this valuable gift of communicating the Good News locally and on social media. In the near future when almost everyone in the world will be connected, our understanding and implementation of evangelism and missions will surely change.

Here in Ephesians 4 Paul highlights "pastors and teachers" as the two leading gifts of the Lord to His Church, with the express directive to shape believers "to the measure of the stature of the fullness of Christ." Pastors and teachers are prominently positioned in our North American church model, with much influence and authority. Those with these gifts should thus be reminded of Jesus's words "to whom much is given, from him much will be required" (Lk. 12:48). Our pastors and teachers must intently engage in discerning and developing those under their care whom the Lord has also gifted. SC requires of them to equip "the saints for the work of ministry." One commentary on Ephesians 4 explains:

> Paul insists that Christ grants gifts to his people upon their entrance into the church. The church functions well because of his gracious gifts, not as a result of the natural talents and abilities of its members - a point well worth remembering. From this, we learn that Christ has gifted *all* believers. Paul will go on to identify specific leadership gifts given to specific persons.[62]

A great opportunity presents itself for our contemporary pastors and teachers to identify God's gifts and develop them as part of their ministries for strengthening their fellowships and for social media platforms. At least annually, consistently, and with the believers' anticipation, a faith community should facilitate a seminar on identifying, promoting, and deploying its God given

---

[62] William W. Klein, *The Expositor's Bible Commentary: Ephesians-Philemon*, Tremper Longman III, David E. Garland, eds. Vol. 12 (Grand Rapids: Zondervan, 2006), 111. Italics used for "all" are from the commentary.

gifts. Messages on the topic should also be preached prior to the seminar, encouraging believers to explore their giftedness.

The endeavours should also break away from the selfie culture and not categorize any gifts by the measurement of what will or what will not contribute to increasing the popularity of the ministry. This temptation of numerical ambition in deploying giftedness is embedded in our carnal nature and remains an ongoing battle, especially in a culture wherein seeking affirmation by popularity is paramount. Even the early Christians were cautioned to beware of creating a community mindset whereby some gifts were respected above others. As Paul cautioned,

> For I say, through the grace given to me, to everyone who is among you, not to think of himself more highly than he ought to think, but to think soberly, as God has dealt to each one a measure of faith. For as we have many members in one body, but all the members do not have the same function, so we, being many, are one body in Christ, and individually members of one another. Having then gifts differing according to the grace that is given to us, let us use them (Rom. 12:3-6).

From Paul's writings we learn how engaging the gifts of all believers is of utmost importance, a duty of a faith community pursuing SC.

What is so interesting is that when Paul wrote a second letter to his protege, Timothy, he reminded him "to stir up the gift of God which is in you" (2:6). Paul then immediately followed with, "For God has not given us a spirit of fear, but of power and of love and of a sound mind" (2:7). Why did Paul encourage Timothy to engage his gift without any fear? Likewise, in 1 Timothy, Paul encouraged him not to let anyone "despise your youth" (4:12).

There are growing generational gaps in our midst where sometimes Elders believe their tenures in CF should usurp authority over the giftedness of younger believers. Power struggles were a reality in Paul's day, and they are in play today as well. For Timothy, some "despised his youth." How often have gifted believers been discouraged by excuses brought their way? "You don't have the experience." "You're not ready yet." "Now is not the time." "Wait for a while." "That is not how it works." "Do this first, and then we'll see." "You have to learn to be a team player." Such excuses are often an attempt to control God's gifts in our midst. Again, we can always opt to facilitate all the gifts God has bestowed to our fellowships. As the human body cannot function optimally unless all of its parts are in good working order so likewise our fellowships cannot achieve an optimal experience of SC unless all of God's gifts among us are utilized.

Part of a Christian's growth in grace is to discover God's gift and to serve and strengthen the ministry of their fellowship. Overall engagement in church will rise, and lifestyle discipleship will be more fulfilling, when believers' gifts are acknowledged and implemented. Whether it's communicating online, administration, worship, visitations, leadership, financial stewardship, church governance, youth programs, hospitality, writing, advising, teaching, counselling, or other areas of giftedness, a fellowship thrives when it's doing what God has gifted everyone to do. Why not purpose to explore these gifted resources in your faith community and commit to creating space for each one?

A valuable lesson here is learned from the experience of Francis Chan when he pastored a megachurch. He recently wrote a book, *Letters to the Church*, wherein he commented:

The Bible tells us that every member of the body has a gift necessary to the functioning of the Church. When I looked at what went on at Cornerstone, I saw a few other people and me using our gifts, while thousands just came and sat in the sanctuary for an hour and a half and then went home. The way we had structured the church was stunting people's growth, and the whole body was weaker for it. It was humbling to discuss biblical commands we had neglected. We decided we wanted to bring change into the church.[63]

Next Sunday, I challenge pastoral leaders to glance over all your congregants and see how many gifts you recognize which are being neglected in your fellowships. You will surely spot many who could be exercising a gift in service to your fellowship, but are sitting there idling week after week. Even worse, we sometimes pay third party vendors for services that could have been performed quite satisfactorily and gratis by those particularly gifted among us. Church leaders are underestimating the gifts God has provided in our midst for the purpose of building one another in CF. We are responsible for how this generation of Christians are encouraged and developed for ministry, both offline and online.

Should we neglect to instruct and develop God's gifts among us then future generations will have a far different experience of church. Out of frustration those who are seeking to deepen their CF will retreat with their gifts and establish unconventional models of fellowship, possibly becoming a reprimanding voice online of

---

[63] Francis Chan, *Letters to the Church* (Colorado Springs: David C. Cook, 2018), 6.

the current models. "Full-time" ministry may no longer have the same meaning as it does today, because financial support will diminish as emerging ministries practice fellowship differently. Personal devices and social media will make it easy for them to plan when and where to fellowship. I am sure there will be an App for that! This potential is now being sown as many bright and gifted believers are sitting idle in our fellowships. Gifted Christians who are not serving with what they are passionate about will become increasingly bored and disengaged. Online platforms are providing opportunities for anyone to express themselves, and if gifted believers are idle in their local faith community it will only be a matter of time until they become creative with social media.

As social beings, believers will continue to seek fellowship and to exchange conversation on their experiences of CF. They will also become increasingly conversant with web analytics, and their reach will become ever more astounding. So how they will meet, where they will meet, the frequencies, and how they will teach SC, could all look far different from our current generation's experience of church. How we teach and develop giftedness today could determine how a community of faith will conduct future ministry. If we condition our generation of believers, even indirectly, on pursuing their individual gifts outside of a fellowship then we are encouraging future trends that could influence many to miss out on experiencing the beauty of harmony in Christian growth and fellowship. Growing in "the unity of faith" is a distinct doctrine of SC which now more than ever requires everyone's contributions.

A pastor friend of mine once asked me if I knew the meaning of "ego"? I thought I did, but he enlightened me. He explained that ego means *edging God out*. Then I understood. When we focus on popularity and neglect the spiritual development of all believers, we are edging God out, and boosting individual profiles. The quest for popularity is sadly influencing many believers to pursue and achieve a celebrity status with their giftedness, which in reality is make-believe. Note how a contemporary Christian leader referred to this generation of believers as "deceived" by "the popularity gospel":

> I have a friend who once said that if the primary deception of our parents' generation was the prosperity gospel, the primary deception of our generation is the popularity gospel. . . . we are taught that the evidence of God's hand on someone's life or ministry is their popularity, how many people they are reaching, how many people come to their church and follow them on social media. . . . There is this misunderstanding that I think has crept into the Church that we would call the 'fear of the spirit of man' that has deceived us into believing that God's will for our lives is that we be popular or influential. The heroes and fathers of our faith, many of them could not have been described as popular or influential. But they were faithful and they feared God.[64]

---

[64] Samuel Smith, "'Popularity gospel' is today's 'prosperity gospel': former Christian music star on how to fear God," *The Christian Post* (January 9, 2019): Online, *https://www.christianpost.com/books/popularity-gospel-is-todays-prosperity-gospel-former-christian-music-star-on-how-to-fear-god.html.* The citation was part of an answer given by Mattie Montgomery in interview

What we are doing is creating a perception of spirituality where a deep experience of CF is tied into one's *star power*. Believers are being conditioned to think that God's affirmation on a ministry is verified by its popularity, and by an impressive following on social media.

This mentality must be discarded if we are to seek a genuine and deep experience of CF and to communicate SC effectively on social media. Regrettably, popularity is determining the validity of one's giftedness and so the unpopular are not perceived as gifted. What then of those believers who are faithfully serving with their gifts but not becoming popular? Are they not communicating a deeper experience of SC because their popularity is not rising? This erroneous implication has become a typical, though subtle, understanding in our faith communities. It is becoming quite sad.

Could anyone possibly imagine a place where the most gifted Christian leaders are not only unpopular, but also anonymous? Where the attention is all on Jesus and His work among believers? Where resources are not dispensed on promoting the gifts of a select few? There is an actual place where God's gifts are having great impact without a popularity gauge, China. Our North American lifestyles of ministry should learn a few lessons from our Chinese brothers and sisters. When Francis Chan resigned in 2010, he visited China, and his experience there was noted recently in *Charisma*:

---

with Smith on his recent book, *Scary God: Introducing the Fear of the Lord to the Postmodern Church* (Nashville: Thomas Nelson, 2018).

While there, he learned a powerful lesson from China's underground movement. The attention-phobic humility of the Chinese church stood in stark contrast to the United States' megachurches and celebrity pastors. Chan recalls one of the Chinese believers telling him: 'The most influential people in the underground church are the most hidden. No one can know who they are.'. . . 'In America, you feel like you need to become famous in order to have impact,' he says. 'But in China it was quite the opposite. . . . It was so cool. The Lord doesn't need our popularity or platform.' As he returned home months later, Chan reflected on what it meant to truly live in ministry.[65]

This should be an eyeopener for all of us. Now it is true "the Lord doesn't need our popularity or platform," but social media is here to stay and so we should take a valuable lesson from the Asian implementation of God's gifts and translate a bit of that approach to our ministries. The underground church in China is flourishing without attention to individuals. They have learned not to *edge God out*. Jesus is truly increasing in their fellowships, as the emphasis on ministry is each believer's growth in "the measure of the stature of the fullness of Christ." Consider us here in North America how far ahead everyone would be in CF if we adapted some of those Asian learnings? How much more impact would our ministries have in our culture if everyone with an online presence were "increasing" Jesus and "decreasing" self? According to SC, our ministerial gifts

---

[65] Taylor Berglund, "The Greatest Commandments: How Francis Chan's radical return to Christian roots is reshaping his faith community," *Charisma* (April 2018): 22-28.

are supplied by God and purposed so "that in all things God may be glorified through Jesus Christ . . . forever and ever" (1 Pet. 4:11).

In this culture of self-centeredness, however, the *w i i f m* factor is nearly uncontrollable (i. e., what's in it for me?)? It's an ageless human desire of the natural person. From the beginning it's what Adam and Eve wanted in the Garden of Eden. They wanted something for themselves, rather than to rely completely on God and His commandments for everything. That is where idolatry originated. We all continue to believe that Jesus should be glorified. Let us therefore refresh our understanding of what it means in our lives and fellowships to glorify Jesus. First, let us be reminded from the beginning that God "breathed" into us "the breath of life" and we "became . . . living being(s)" (Gen. 2:7). Then we *all* sinned, messed up, made grievous mistakes, hurt one another, failed miserably in our relationships, and fallen "short of the glory of God" (Rom. 3:23). Yet God, "who is rich in mercy, because of His great love with which He loved us, even when we were dead in trespasses, made us alive together with Christ (by grace you have been saved)" (Eph. 2:4-5). Our CF originated from the grace of God to us. What could we possibly expect in addition for ourselves? Our personal experience of salvation is on account of Jesus. Our gifts were bestowed by Him. How could any recipient of such grace even consider, "What's in it for me?" Even if we completely obeyed our Lord, we would still have no claim to anything. For Jesus said, "So likewise you, when you have done all these things which you are commanded say, 'We are unprofitable servants, We have done what was our duty to do'" (Lk. 17:10).

Honestly put, Jesus is not satisfying enough to those who are irresistibly promoting self. They require the fulfillment provided by popularity. That is why I emphasized markedly in the previous chapter how Jesus *must* be truly fulfilling in our lives if we are to experience the depths of SC and engage effectively within culture. We shouldn't be naive and think that our God given gifts are always communicating Jesus with altruistic intentions. The nature of ministry today makes it easy to draw unhealthy attention to oneself while maintaining the guise of spirituality. What I am about to note is not generally applicable to the ministries of all successful and gifted communicators of SC. It nevertheless remains necessary to mention because there is evidently a growing problem that some Christians should be made aware of before their faith and lives suffer irreparable damage.

Incredibly, a recent research project revealed that there is an epidemic of narcissism in the North American church. Two years ago, an exhaustive study was undertaken on the topic and the authors noted a dramatic presence of narcissism in our churches, naming it "the plague." In *Let us Prey* they wrote,

> We expect many things of our pastors. In particular, the commandments of Jesus about loving one another is problematic to the narcissist. 'You shall love your neighbours as yourself' (Matt. 19:19) and 'Do to others as you would have them do to you' (Lk. 6:31) are just part of the pastoral job description. Unfortunately, they are foreign and even incomprehensible to the narcissist. They will recite 'love your

neighbour' convincingly and often, but really have no idea of what that form of love is.[66]

The number of leaders these researchers diagnosed with narcissistic tendencies is alarming. Needless to say, where such self-glorification is present there will be an absence of focus on glorifying Jesus. Grandstanding with one's gift in a fellowship obfuscates the communication and flow of a deeper CF, missing the substance of SC. Our hearts and prayers should truly go out to all those who are under such leadership. May God truly strengthen them, and if it were me I would flee immediately. We were warned a long time ago by the Apostle Paul "that in the last days perilous times will come. *For men will be lovers of themselves*" (2 Tim. 3:1-2). There has never been an era such as this where so many people are becoming irresistibly drawn to seek attention to themselves.

Surely, we are all nodding our heads to affirm the import of Paul's warning. Unless we exercise individual Christian discipline as noted in the previous chapter, one's temptation to promote self and pursue popularity in ministry will be extremely difficult to overcome. I am sincerely concerned about this challenge going forward: *extremely difficult to overcome.* Our fascination with social media popularity could potentially decrease the pristine intentions of SC and establish a wave of activity that fuels and establishes the "popularity Gospel." Like Martha's sister Mary we must begin at

---

[66] Glenn Ball and Darrell Puts, *Let Us Prey: The Plague of Narcissist Pastors and What We Can Do About It* (Eugene, Oregon: Cascade Books, 2017), 48. The book includes a helpful guide for pastoral search committees, with a list of must ask questions which will reveal any narcissistic tendencies in a prospective candidate.

the feet of Jesus. You, me, all of us, must get to know Him, and *know* Him well. Then we will communicate our giftedness to make remarkable impact in culture.

As Jesus increases in our lives, we will become happier with a lifestyle of discipleship that prioritizes SC. How we rank on the popularity scale will shrink in appeal, and spiritually healthier relationships will be established with one another. Less focus will be placed on how many followers we have on social media, with more focus on how we are learning and growing in SC. We can talk about love for others, humility, and communication of God's grace. We can preach about it; we can write about it; we can read and study about it; we can teach it all day long, but unless Jesus increases in one's life it will not be humanly possible for many to overcome in this era of selfies. I would encourage you to begin to focus on deepening your relationship with Jesus and decreasing the time you spend gauging your popularity status online. Unless we increase in our personal fulfillment of Jesus it will be excruciatingly difficult to teach like John the Baptist, "He must increase, but I must decrease."

Perhaps it is time to diminish the frequencies of checking our social media accounts. If you are accustomed to checking the action hourly, can you reduce it to once or twice a day? It will be painful at first, but the practice will begin to reveal to you what SC is all about as you focus less on your popularity and experience more of the heavenly fulfillment Jesus really does provide. Popularity can be quite gratifying, but its pursuit can affect our family lives, work productivity, offline ministries, relationships, and cause us to read less. Deepening your relationship with Jesus is what will provide ongoing strength to overcome the unrelenting barrage of temptations encountered at an instant click. A believer's increasing popularity online can never provide the substance required to live peacefully, joyfully, and to exercise maximum influence in offline ministry. In short, an insatiable desire for popularity can be a menace to one's spiritual well-being and maturing process in SC. Nevertheless, do not be discouraged!

Where do you see yourself communicating God's giftedness? Offline? Online? Both? What are you most passionate about in ministry? Note, however, that sometimes an encouraging or discouraging word about your gift by one of your peers or leaders is not necessarily final. Input from others is integral to a Christian's development in ministerial gifts, but ultimately it is between you and God. In your heart, you will know your gift and service to the family of God and beyond. It is as if you cannot see yourself doing anything else, regardless of what others comment about you. "For if I preach the gospel," said Paul, "I have nothing to boast of, for *necessity is laid upon me*; yes, woe is me if I do not preach the gospel!" (1 Cor. 9:16). You may be interested to know that even back then Paul's gifts were evaluated and even questioned by some. As he received feedback, "'For his letters,' they say, 'are weighty and powerful, but his bodily presence is weak, and his speech contemptible.'" (2 Cor. 10:10). Your God given gift should be treasured by you, and regardless of what anyone says you should remain determined to its use and seek to edify others, both offline and online. I have known some employed in full-time ministry who enjoyed utilizing their gifts so much that if it were possible, they would serve without pay. Conversely, you will experience frustration when something prevents you from serving in the role you are most passionate about.

If you are a gifted musician then you should seek to become the most God inspired musician you can possibly be. If you are a preacher do not seek to imitate anyone except to grow in your God given uniqueness. Seek to be clay in the Potter's hands. Do not concern yourself with criticisms that pressure you to be other than what God intends. Same goes if you are an administrator, teacher, evangelist, or hospitality provider. Compete with no one except yourself, and let the Lord be your inspiration. The purpose of giftedness is to serve with integrity and to seek ultimate satisfaction in how the Spirit is developing you to minister with great influence. When this process is active there will be no need to compete with anyone or to seek popularity. You will be enjoying the promised "abundant life" so much that you will really wish for others to excel and to "stir their gifts." Nevertheless, if God does make you to become widely known, and it is quite possible in today's world, you will be a great blessing to many. Personally, a great delight of mine is to listen to a speaker that is uniquely gifted by God and deliver substance. When I read a Christian blog online that leaps out with resonant SC I am greatly encouraged. Can you appreciate a fellowship where everyone is serving and Jesus is truly worshipped as the "High Priest" (Heb. 4:15) and we all perceive ourselves as a "chosen generation, a royal priesthood, a holy nation, His own special people" (1 Pet. 2:9)?

Don't you wish you could truly love your brothers and sisters and see them excel with their gifts? Don't you wish there was space in your faith community for everyone to exercise their gifts? Don't you wish you could wholeheartedly celebrate the achievements of those similarly gifted as you? If by chance you were to answer no to these questions, or with a slow and reluctant yes without any compunction, then I encourage you to freshen your understanding of giftedness and provide more space for Jesus in your life. Ironically, almost everyone today continues to appeal to the authority of the Bible. We hear it often: "that's not biblical," or, "show me where that is in the Bible." Let us learn yet another lesson directly from the Scriptures. Paul taught clearly, "Let each of you look not only for his own interests, but also for the interests of others. Let this mind be in you which was also in Christ Jesus" (Philip. 2: 4-5). Seriously? Are we to "look . . . for the interests of others"? "*Of others,*" in a culture of selfies? Indeed, this is SC. This is part of being a deep Christian thinker, to think genuinely and seriously about serving others with our gifts.

His increasing presence in your life will become so real that you will be sensitive to grieving the Spirit when seeking to increase yourself. By increasing in Him you will also learn from the Spirit that the depths of SC release God's wisdom, which is indispensable in discerning today's culture. In James we read,

> But if you have bitter envy and self-seeking in your hearts, do not boast and lie against the truth. This wisdom does not descend from above, but is earthly, sensual, demonic. For where envy and self-seeking exist, confusion and every evil thing are there. But the wisdom that is from above is first pure, then peaceable, gentle, willing to lead, full of mercy and good fruits, without partiality and without hypocrisy (Jam. 3: 14-18).

When God's gifts are "self-seeking" there is an absence of "heavenly wisdom." God's gifts are purposed with specificity, particularly to build up His people. James also writes, "Do not be deceived, my beloved brethren. Every good gift and every perfect gift is from above, and comes down from the Father of lights, with whom there is no variation or shadow of turning" (Jam. 1:16-17). This teaching is consistent in SC. Nonetheless exercising our gifts selflessly in today's culture is also as difficult as "loving your enemies." They are equally impossible to accomplish on our own. In other words, they are both unnatural inclinations but they remain Scriptural injunctions.

Social media make it challenging to teach SC, because the inner logic of social media is to encourage copious communications without filters or fact checking mechanisms. Thankfully there are scholars who are gifted with exceptional theological insight and have received a golden opportunity to communicate their giftedness on social media. Yet even such communication requires development in a culture of online communication. For example, Andrew Byers writes,

> Twitter's apparent anxiety over my tweet lessness and WordPress's enthusiasm over my pressing of words are about *activity*, not *content*. Neither of these fine and upstanding companies are weighing the validity of my blog posts or my occasional tweets based on their theological integrity or stylistic sophistication. 'Just write.' But just write *what?* Anything? Just write . . . because writing creates posts, and posts create traffic. Traffic is activity. And somewhere down the road for a dot-com, activity is income.[67]

SC requires careful and thoughtful communications and the encouragement to "just write" increases subtly the margin for

---

[67] Andrew Byers, *TheoMedia: The Media of God and the Digital Age* (Eugene, OR: Cascade Books, 2013), 20.

popularity at every level. Even our gifted theologians need all the spiritual strength available in Him if they are to serve and overcome in this culture of self. None of our gifts are immune to the inclinations towards popularity.

Power to overcome is found in the fulfillment of Jesus. Even so, Nehemiah encouraged in the Old Testament, "The joy of the Lord is your strength" (Neh. 8:10). His joy is truly unlike anything else, and those who have experienced its depths know how vital it is to a fulfilling Christian life. No amount of skill, theological education, or popularity on social media, can substitute for the strength found in His joy. Like loving your enemies, you cannot do it unless your soul is fulfilled by Jesus. We need to remain steadfast in CF, because there is much to accomplish going forward. Even with all of our giftedness we are not winning, but increasingly "losing influence" over mainstream culture in North America. In *The Great Evangelical Recession*, award winning journalist and Pastor, John S. Dickerson writes:

> We are losing influence because the host culture is changing so much faster than we (or even it) can understand . . . We are losing influence because culture at large is realizing, formally or informally, that evangelicals are not as big or significant as we have claimed. Whether by percent of population, power of vote, or simple cultural influence, we are no longer as mighty as we once were.[68]

---

[68] John S. Dickerson, *The Great Evangelical Recession: 6 Factors That Will Crash the American Church . . . and How to Prepare* (Grand Rapids: BakerBooks, 2013), 26.

Being born and raised in Canada, I can comment informatively that the loss of impact over culture is an even bigger issue for Canadian evangelicals. In North America, we are not living as a community of believers that reflects an influential witness consistently. A main reason is that we have failed to appreciate one another's gifts and have not sought to develop them. We have become fragmented as each believer seeks to communicate his or her own giftedness, with hardly any attention on developing those of others in our fellowships. We are therefore not as fortified as we should be in order to engage culture effectively.

Social media will definitely play a role as we continue to "press" towards "the goal for the prize of the upward call of God in Christ Jesus" (Philip. 3:14). Ministries ought to focus more on mobilizing others rather than fixating on numerical metrics that seek to aggrandize self. Thankfully, Christian leaders are beginning to acknowledge that God's given resources to the church should be developed in order to make significant contributions in their societies. In *The Next Christians*, Gabe Lyons noted pastors who "are mobilizing entire congregations *to use their gifts and talents* to solve real problems in their communities."[69] Identifying the vast resources of God's gifts among us is indispensable to affecting people in meaningful ways. Let us proceed with confidence, for it is an exciting time to be communicating with God's giftedness.

---

[69] Gabe Lyons, *The Next Christians: The Good News About the End of Christian America* (New York: DoubleDay, 2010), 201-02. Italics in citation are mine and used for emphasis.

Our CF can be equipped to rise above a secular culture and communicate its relevancy.

Chapter 4

LIFESTYLE DISCIPLESHIP IN A CULTURE OF SCRIPTURAL INDIFFERENCE

"Go therefore and make disciples of all the nations . . . teaching them to observe all things that I have commanded you" Matthew 28:19-20

Another reason why evangelicals are losing influence is because they are assimilating into North American cultural thought without significant discernment. Every once in a while, we remind ourselves of the often quoted Scripture in Romans: "be transformed by the renewing of your mind, that you may prove what is that good and acceptable and perfect will of God" (12:2). Yet our thinking is identifying increasingly with mainstream culture. Think about it: Is there anything observably special about contemporary evangelicals?

We live in various neighbourhoods with homes like everyone else. We drive the same cars, wear the same brands, and shop at the same stores. Vocationally, we pursue similar career paths as everyone else and most are always striving to make more money. Financial planning is part of our household as it is in everyone else's. We give financially to our fellowships, but our non-Christian friends and neighbours also give to worthwhile charities. Our children attend the same local schools; some attend private secular schools and some attend private Christian schools. Christian parents have the highest aspirations for their children and are as competitive as non-Christian parents. Everyone watches the same television programs, movies, sports events, and listens to the same music, albeit with some discretion here and there. We go out for dinner to the same restaurants and enjoy the same entertainment venues. We even throw Super Bowl parties and indulge ourselves no differently from our unbelieving neighbours. There is one notable distinction, however. On Sunday mornings our neighbours can observe us huddling in our vehicles and going to church.

You are probably thinking, yes, but what distinguishes us from non-Christians is our acceptance of God's grace. That is true. Moreover, God expects us to be responsible and productive stewards and to contribute to our societies and facilitate community. Even so, we need to earn our keep and support our families. Yes, these are also correct and noble pursuits. Moreover, we are simply living out our CF and enjoying all that God gave us. Sure, we are to enjoy God's blessings. However, as we go about our daily business, and engage with culture shouldn't our affections be informed from above? "Set your mind on things above" wrote Paul, "not on things on the earth" (Col. 3:2). John also said: "Do not love the world or the things in the world. If anyone loves the world, the love of the Father is not in him" (1 Jn. 2:15). We should admit to ourselves that by observing our lives apart from Sunday mornings we are pretty much like everyone else.

Honestly, who among us is really living John's command, "Do not love the world or the things in the world?" We can analyze this text with exegetical gymnastics and produce manifold interpretations to suit however we wish for it to apply to ourselves. Remember that SC seeks to understand the intended meaning of the ageless message of the biblical writers and not what we would like it to mean in order to accommodate ourselves. My point is that our experience of CF should impel us to seek ways to influence culture effectively, and not the other way around. First of all, we should not be pressured to interpret SC to accommodate what cultural thought would possibly consider acceptable. Our CF has placed us in an extraordinarily special relationship with God, and we should allow that relationship to guide us. We must acknowledge the richness of Scriptural descriptions about us as the people of God, and then we can begin to understand what it is we are desiring for other people.

What makes Christians Scripturally distinct as "royal," as part of "a chosen generation," and as "special" to Jesus (1 Pet. 2:9), "is the true grace of God" in us (1 Pet. 5:12). "If indeed you have tasted that the Lord is gracious" (1 Pet. 2:3), you will possess deep convictions about the character of Jesus, about your call to discipleship, and how you ought to engage with everyone. Sometimes we shy away from expressing our Scriptural convictions, because we know that cultural thought disapproves and causes us to be embarrassed. I am not referring to anything to do with my earlier discussion on "legalism" in Chapter 2. I am referring here to my earlier question from one believer to another in Chapter 1 (What have you been learning from the Lord Jesus lately?). Of course, if you were to ask someone at the mall that same question it would be inappropriate and deemed weird. The question, however, was considered in the context of a faith community foyer after Sunday morning worship, after affirming the teaching of Jesus as Lord, and after giving financial support to the work of discipleship. Our convictions reveal that we are part of a "royal" family of God, having experienced His special grace and are consciously part of "a chosen generation." So why has that question become weird to many believers even in the context of a worship centre?

What characterizes our North American culture is "the lust of the flesh, the lust of the eyes, and the pride of life" (1 Jn. 2:16), and these are forces everywhere tempting a believer. Cultural thought has affected all of us. We try to resist cultural trends that are contrary to our beliefs in SC, but they are in some degree part of our lives. This is the reality of the context in which we attempt to exercise a lifestyle of discipleship. Some believers identify with culture more than others and some with certain aspects of it, but we are all embracing one thing or the other from culture. In fact, we cannot express our lifestyle discipleship by avoiding our culture. Our lives cannot be separated from culture as if we speak or live in a manner that is completely detached from it, for we are endeavouring to remain *relevant*. While we attempt to stay in the conversation, it is important to note that our claim to Truth should not cause us consternation when cultural thought tells us that our language is not inclusive enough.

Cultural thought now perceives any claim to Christian absolutism as arrogant, and our conversation as time-warped. Christians are thus pressured to think far more liberally, or keep their convictions to themselves. Culture's general insinuation at best, when not critical towards CF, is that it's the same as any other religious belief. Pluralism is a cherished cultural value and thus SC's staunchly monistic message is not appreciated. Know this with certainty that all religions are not the same. They do not all teach the same thing. SC is unique because it alone provides real forgiveness by God's Saviour, and grace can be experienced with the onset of a "new birth." Humankind is not required to do

140

anything to merit favour from God. The Spirit indwells a repentant believer who has accepted His grace, and Jesus becomes a personal Friend. No other religion teaches this. It's not arrogant because the invitation is open to all. Yet culture is affecting all believers to some degree, and so we are becoming reluctant to talk about our CF, even in the foyer of our fellowships.

Private clubs are more along the lines of arrogant because not all can join. You must first satisfy particular criteria and then you must be approved by the club's leaders. Christianity is not a private club, because all are invited to accept His grace. SC is completely inclusive as the Saviour welcomes everyone indiscriminately, and imparts unconditional grace to all those who ask for forgiveness: "There is neither Jew nor Greek, there is neither slave nor free, there is neither male nor female; for you are all one in Christ Jesus" (Gal. 3:28). Even so, God loves and invites all to accept His grace: "For there is no partiality with God" (Rom. 2:11).

Yet the exclusive claims of CF and talk of Jesus as "the way, the truth, and the life" have become indifferent to cultural consciousness. What irks culture about the CF is precisely the claims to exclusivity and how they make implications that interrupt people's self-seeking agendas. CF calls for repentance; it condemns sin; it worships only Jesus, and even highly educated and sophisticated people comply. Like everyone else Christians are part of a wider culture and we become aware that claims of SC are not welcomed. Consequently, talk of SC is being pressured not to offend any part of established cultural thought, and the pressure has also crossed over to affect conversations between believers. Accommodating the expectations of the culture has affected how we express our inner most convictions of our undeniable experience of God's grace. We continue to be gripped by what Paul wrote in Romans: "The Spirit Himself bears witness with our spirit that we are children of God" (8:16), but we internalize our experience of CF and adjust our outward affections to cultural norms and practices. Insomuch that if we were to ask one another in the halls of our own fellowships - What have you been learning from the Lord Jesus lately? - we would consider it a weird question because the culture we all live and move in considers it so. Believers' convictions of CF are being silenced by cultural thought and relegated to the private and internal sphere of being.

Our affections are not far different from everyone else we interact with, and so we are not critical enough of cultural trends that attempt to silence SC. Inside of our church sanctuaries we are completely engaged with the worship, the sermon, our greeting of one another, and even in our financial giving. When we step out, even into the foyer, cultural thought takes over. We begin to talk, share, and communicate all of our material affections and experiences which outweigh our desire for one another to be more like Jesus. Cultural thought has influenced us more than we care to realize, whereas we should be growing in our convictions of CF and not think that we will hurl condemnations if we engage culture with them. Even though we practice our CF within cultural norms it should not mean that we ought to harmonize SC with cultural thought.

Culture seems to have an erroneous view that SC is full of condemnations. How they got those assumptions is a discussion for another day. Let us learn from what our Master said in one of His conversations with a habitual adulteress: "Neither do I condemn you; go and sin no more" (Jn. 8:11). "For God did not send His Son into the world to condemn the world" (Jn. 3:17). What we need to know and experience is that, "He who does not love does not know God, for God is love" (1 Jn. 4:8). Loving God and loving others cannot be separated. When gripped by this verse people around us will know unmistakably that we care; that we are not arrogant; that our CF is not about hurling condemnations; that we are inviting all; and most of all, we will have strength to engage cultural thought's misinformed judgements of SC. A genuine exploration of SC will reveal Jesus as gracious, forgiving, and loving humankind to the point of sacrificing Himself for them.

Remember the exercise in Chapter 2 where you stood at a safe spot at a busy intersection and watched people? After an experience of God's grace, a believer will see people with a newly found glowing love, and not with condemning eyes. Your worldview is also especially different as your sense of *knowingness* of "the Truth" *affects* how you understand people, relationships, friendships, family, career, education, giftedness, and everything else. No doubt that a growing appetite to communicate the Good News emanates from one's own unmistakable experience of transformation by grace. As C. S. Lewis said, "I believe in Christianity as I believe that the Sun has risen, not only because I see it, but because by it I see everything else."[70] Your life becomes characterized by a regenerated relationship with God, and you know deep within that only Jesus can provide real forgiveness and

---

[70] C. S. Lewis, *Is Theology Poetry* (essay presented at the Oxford Socratic Club, November 6, 1944).

heal brokenness for all people. You will then desire to make a difference in the lives of those around you.

A growing experience of SC will also reveal an enjoyment of holiness, yes, *holiness*. Another one of those terms that is considered embarrassing in contemporary culture. When was the last time you heard a solid teaching on holiness? SC commands us to "Pursue peace with all people, *and holiness*, without which no one will see the Lord" (Heb. 12:14). Likewise, "as He who called you is holy, you also be holy in all your conduct, because it is written, 'Be holy, for I am holy'" (1 Pet. 1:15). That may sound absurd to many in this culture, and even anachronistic to others, but it is SC. Remember what was noted earlier that SC will never become popular, so neither will holiness. We are called to be set apart for God in order to live an influential lifestyle of discipleship. This separation, however, causes tension between us and cultural thought with which we interact daily.

Holiness is sadly misunderstood even by many believers. It is not a life of piety belonging to a bygone era; nor should it be understood as a lifestyle of unrealistic expectations for our frenzied lifestyles. Holiness should be understood as a progression in the "abundant life" promised by Jesus. A current reflection puts it this way,

> Some people remain confused by thinking that holiness is unattainable. They wrongly believe that holiness sets the bar too high. If it is the high road, it seems too steep and exhausting. It requires a spiritual stamina beyond one's capacity. The Bible is clear that God's desire is that all persons experience a full salvation from the guilt and penalty of sin and to having power over sin, growing in grace and Christlikeness,

and being filled with the fullness of God. These ideals seem to remain attainable.[71]

What is impeding our quest for holiness is how culture erodes its pursuit by an accentuated expression of "the lust of the eyes and the lust of the flesh" in film, television, online, and huge billboards everywhere. Many believers are now accustomed to living with graphic images of sex, material pursuits, and hearing profane language, without any qualms. It's all part of the culture now. Even a believer's standards for what counts as impropriety have decreased dramatically. Thus, if believers are to take holiness seriously, they will experience tension within culture. As SC confirms, "Yes, and all who desire to live godly in Christ Jesus will suffer persecution" (2 Tim. 3:12). Holiness remains an inward desire despite how our culture is ignorant of its values. We must understand holiness not as merely a tenet of CF, nor as a dictatorial imposition by God, but as part of a growing, learning, and fulfilling relationship with Jesus. A life set apart for God will continue to interact with cultural trends, but it will do so with keen discernment and power to maintain a lifestyle of devotion to Him. We must begin by deciding that as God's people we will break through these cultural barriers, for He has given us the strength.

Let us reflect solemnly on what Jesus revealed to us when he said, "I am the light of the world. He who follows Me shall not walk in darkness but have the light of life" (Jn. 8:12). You should read this and understand in a very real way how you experienced

---

[71] Jonathan S. Raymond, *Social Holiness: The Company We Keep* (Aldersgate Press, 2018), 16.

the transition from living in sin to finding strength in Him for a new lifestyle of holiness. You should also know experientially how sin can be dark, and how it imprisons people. Your experience of Jesus rescuing you from the darkness of sin is now very much illustrative of how He became "the Light" in your life. Anyone who has experienced Jesus as "the Light," and overcame the darkness of sin, can appreciate the life changing power of the Gospel in contra-distinction to how cultural thought undermines a lifestyle of holiness. The experience revealed in SC will also relate to you today: "But now being set free from sin, and having become slaves of God, you have your fruit to holiness, and the end, everlasting life" (Rom. 6:22). The depths of SC will also reveal a personal experience similar to what the Psalmist articulated: "How sweet are Your words to my taste, sweeter than honey to my mouth! Through your precepts I get understanding; Therefore, I hate every false way" (Ps. 119: 103-04). Indeed, the Word of God can become very sweet and fulfilling to those who digest it. It discerns what is contrary to holiness and provides strength to overcome. Realistically, we can experience consistently what Paul highlighted in his famous sermon to the culture of his day: "for in Him we live and move and have our being" (Acts 17: 28).

First, we should identify what gives impetus to cultural thought. How are trends established? How does cultural thought manage to suggest effectively how others should think about things? The answer is, *people*. Culture itself is a very broad concept and any Christian study of it that omits to highlight the human condition behind a culture will provide an insufficient understanding, and underestimates a culture's potential. Sure, it is necessary to emphasize and defend the Lordship of Christ, the

Christian life in society, and how institutions need to be called into account. Nevertheless, cultural theology should stress the reality of the fallenness of the *people behind it all*, and the power of God's grace to regenerate people in society. Furthermore, theologizing about the Kingdom of Christ and how it ought to establish its reign over culture is intellectually stimulating for the network of cultural theologians, but it does little for a disciple who slogs 9 to 5 and then goes home to deal with the challenges of life. If we are to bring all to the submission of Christ and defend the legitimacy of the Christian lifestyle in culture, as we should, it must begin with an emphasis on where the hearts and minds of both believers and non-believers are coming from. The experience of a real transition from natural to spiritual by the grace of God remains a fulfilling reality intended for *all people*. That is what a teaching on cultural theology should make clear. Redeemed people will then influence other people in culture.

It is people who influence a cultural trend; whether the material is bogus or not is irrelevant once it becomes in vogue, because as was said in the outset cultural trends can take on a mysterious force. In this milieu, Christians must not only distinguish people from content, and discern Scriptural truth from falsehood, but also strive to make disciples that are "born of God." If we are to engage people effectively then our SC ought to read the culture, discern it, and express our CF in ways that will resonate. As one prolific theological thinker commented:

> In order to be competent proclaimers and performers of the gospel, then Christians must learn to read the Bible and culture alike. Christians cannot afford to continue sleepwalking their way through contemporary culture, letting their lives, and

especially their imaginations, become conformed to culturally devised myths, each of which promises more than it can deliver: 'Do not conform any longer to the pattern of this world, but be transformed by the renewing of your mind' (Rom. 12:2). The apostolic exhortation confronts us with a question: In which cultural world of meaning do *we* dwell? To what pattern have we conformed our imaginations? Will the real world please stand out?[72]

As we live in society, we cannot help but encounter what is being suggested by institutions, film, music, television programs, news outlets, commercials, the arts, literature, political voices, and the fierce skepticism of secularism. Cultural thought thus takes on expression and Christians are not immune to the trends within our context. Once we have assessed cultural trends by SC then our CF in context will be informed, and a lifestyle of discipleship will be far more influential.

Pointing to everything that is wrong with institutions instigates battles. Sometimes it is unavoidable, but if Christians are to extend the Kingdom of God in every area of life then the emphasis should be on knowing Christ as well as the inner longings of a natural person, and then theologize, intellectualize, and mobilize from there. Discipleship should be engaged at every level of society not by declaring war on culture but by discerning it and engaging *people*

---

[72] Kevin J. Vanhoozer, "What Is Everyday Theology? How and Why Christians Should Read Culture" In *Everyday Theology: How to Read Cultural Texts and Interpret Trends*, Kevin J. Vanhoozer, Charles A. Anderson, Michael J. Sleasman, eds. (Grand Rapids: Baker Academic, 2007), 15-62.

with SC. We need to divest our thinking from believing that our mission is to reform institutions, because they are inanimate and thus not the bane of CF. Rather, people who operate institutions require reform and the beauty of the Gospel continues to relate with great satisfaction to an open heart. Teachers and pastors should focus more on the spiritual condition of a natural person, what it values, its potential influences, and how it is establishing cultural trends that are not supporting humanity's quest for fulfillment. When we talk about CF intelligently within our cultural context people will have "ears to hear."

At the beginning of this century Ravi Zacharias had emphasized how church leaders must learn how people think. In *Is Your Church Ready?* he said,

> We must begin by knowing how the mind works and, more to the point, how we must move from thought to action. This demands rigorous practical insight, particularly into the very process by which people come to believe certain things. Some pastors and church leaders may not be given to philosophical thinking, but each of us wrestles with these issues at some level, as surely does our audience.[73]

Zacharias was right and we should have paid closer attention. In culture, secularism is suggesting scorching challenges to our CF and even believers are beginning to think about them and being influenced by them. People now have a far more general

---

[73] Ravi Zacharias, "Four Challenges for Church Leaders" *In Is Your Church Ready?*, Ravi Zacharias and Norman Geisler, eds. (Grand Rapids: Zondervan, 2003), 25-38.

knowledge than previous generations as information is readily available. When newcomers attend our meetings, we can presuppose that they are thinking about the suggestions of secular culture. Our conversation requires engagement with how secularism is influencing people. Preaching, teaching, and one on one discussions, now require a general knowledge of various disciplines if we are to engage effectively with how culture is moving. History, the arts, biblical theology, apologetics, and other disciplines must now be used to illustrate how secularism is essentially a movement of people who have influenced cultural trends that somehow are believed to be more noteworthy than SC. That is how Paul engaged the cultural thought of his day as noted in Acts 17. He discerned the idolatry, referred to poetry, history, and engaged with philosophers. He then presented the risen Christ.

What gives suggestions to a culture for moral, political, and religious thought, is when *human initiative* attempts to influence *other people*. Culture thus takes on a trend when enough people conform to what people behind the suggestion proposed. A practicing trend is then activated in the arena of moral and political discussion, with debates emerging among those who extol and those who criticize. When secular culture espouses a trend, which was influenced by a carnal mind, it can become a challenge for Christian thought. The Gospel should therefore reach people in all walks of life, by Christians in all walks of life, before culture can establish an ungodly trend. There are persons behind every cultural trend and regardless of how powerful, moneyed, or famous, they all have hearts, minds, emotions, feelings, shortcomings, flaws, strengths, weaknesses, and every other human trait. Although now highly counter-cultural, the Gospel was not intended to be communicated to inanimate entities but to human hearts and minds.

In Romans, Paul explained how grace can transform a human being even in the most pagan cultures. His message was not aimed at the powerful institution of Rome, but *"to you who are in Rome."* As he said, "I am ready to preach the gospel *to you who are in Rome* also. For I am not ashamed of the gospel of Christ, for it is the power of God to salvation for *everyone* who believes" (Rom. 1: 15-16). Paul was savvy of the cultural forces of his day and how they could pressure believers to conceal their convictions about Jesus. He thus emphasized the prerequisite of removing the "ashamed" factor in order to release the sure *"power of God to salvation for everyone who believes."* The Gospel's power of grace continues efficaciously today without prejudice towards anyone who believes, and we should not be "ashamed" of such Good News. A lifestyle of discipleship should understand that we are dealing within a culture made not by indomitable forces, but by *humankind.* The foundation for contemporary cultural theology ought to be the Book of Romans wherein Paul unpacks the Christian understanding of law, sin, grace, and the discernment of cultural forces. Cultural theology should contribute to disciple making with an emphasis on the reality of *the human condition* in culture.

By no means is this an ad hominem approach. Rather, natural thinking behind cultural thought should be discerned as incapable of understanding SC meaningfully. The highly influential beliefs of secularism should be understood as void of appreciating what we have experienced as "the light of the world." As Paul also added, "For we walk by faith, not by sight" (2 Cor. 5:7). Cultural trends receive impetus from a human perspective that attempts to naturalize explanations for everything. Cultural thought's naturalistic mind-set has established a worldview that cannot appreciate "justification by faith," "rejoicing in the Lord," and "living for God," because it walks by sight, and hasn't experienced CF. In conversation, therefore, we should realize that much of the criticism towards CF emanates from a spiritually unregenerate mind that requires a listening and discerning ear. Within this cultural milieu we communicate our language of SC, which is becoming increasingly strange to cultured people. Culture asks what Nicodemus asked of Jesus: "How can these things be" (Jn. 3:9)? That is why a lifestyle of discipleship must engage people with words and actions, and allow the Spirit to move people. Perhaps we can learn something from a Christian barber in England who said, "My faith has had more than an impact on my work. Through the conversations I have, a visit to the barbershop can affect someone's image as well as their mind; you get to affect both the inside and the outside. . . People see God through actions."[74]

Indeed, discipleship is a lifestyle that should engage people in meaningful ways by listening, serving, loving, and action. How we talk, listen, serve, work, and interact with people who know we are Christians can make quite a difference. A lifestyle of discipleship is about faithfully exemplifying Christ in whatever we do in society, while understanding where a cultured person is coming from.

Our *knowingness* should, therefore, compel us to live out CF consistently because people evaluate a messenger as much as the

---

[74] Mark Maciver, (barber), "God at Work," *Premiere Christianity* (Jan 2019): 30.

message. In culture, brands have become extremely careful with how their image is being presented. More than ever they are concerned with public perception. They know very well that the people in front of their brand can influence its success or instigate its demise. I remember being in the check-out line of a brand name store and overhearing an exchange between a cashier and a customer. The customer's experience was obviously not good as she left saying, "I am never shopping here again." You see, the brand name may be great but customers do not engage with a sign or an image but with the people who represent the brand. Pressure on brand names to keep up with portraying a great image is now mounting as anyone can criticize anonymously online and easily affect others. Everywhere now the emphasis is on training employees to provide an exceptional customer experience. Brands always encourage feedback after a touch point with a customer, because they are becoming obsessed with public perception. How much more ought we to be concerned with our representation of the Saviour of the world?

In 2 Corinthians, believers were described as *letters* "known and read by all" (3:2). A scholar provides this helpful commentary on the passage: "These images have to do with the ongoing openness of authentic ministry, its public platform as the life of the church plays out before a watching world."[75] CF now means different things to different people. Laser focus, however, is on how devout Christians behave in society. Believers represent their CF "before

---

[75] George H. Guthrie, *2 Corinthians: Baker Exegetical Commentary on the New Testament* (Grand Rapids: Baker Academic, 2015), 189.

a watching world" and their beliefs are evaluated by their actions. In turn, people observe believers through the eyes of cultural thought and they can magically detect inconsistencies in a lifestyle of discipleship. Though the attention of people on Christians is latent, it nevertheless is quick to pass evaluations and become increasingly turned off by witnessing hypocrisy. What would make anyone desire our CF except for how we exercise a lifestyle of discipleship?

This is why the prosperity Gospel has failed miserably. Prosperity preachers have a flawed understanding of SC as they promote material things from God as a confirmation of His blessings on a believer's CF. By implication, and promoted seriously by staunch proponents, if believers are not receiving material blessings from God then there is something wrong with their CF. This message is damaging on so many levels, and cultural thought is quick to tear it up. Furthermore, prosperity preachers promoted material prosperity as a manner in which God provided fulfillment to His faithful. Focusing on material things as the object of fulfillment is not what the revealed grace of God in SC is all about. The Gospel is about people communicating God's grace to other people, not the promotion of material things. "For in Him," wrote Paul, "dwells all the fullness of the Godhead bodily; and you are complete in Him" (Col. 2: 9-10). Prosperity preachers brought SC in disrepute in culture by the stark contrast between what Jesus taught and their own inordinately lavish lifestyles. Enormous backfire developed in cultural thought which continues to linger today. Documentaries, movies, and literature, have disparaged CF on account of how the prosperity Gospel fleeced people and enriched the leaders. This stigma on CF has entered into cultural consciousness, and remains indelibly stamped in mainstream culture.

Yet some believe that culture has a life of its own. In other words, cultural trends can transcend what was intended and sweep through a society. Others believe that culture can become systemic and not reducible to human actions. I disagree, because the human constitution is self-determinate. Choices are always available. Every cultural trend has always had counter-cultural people who exercised resistance. The Nazis, for example, managed to create a culture of anti-Semitism through its nefarious propaganda machine. There were those, however, who admirably discerned the cultural thinking as evil and helped Jewish people even at the threat of severe penalty. In the sixties, the sexual revolution created a culture of promiscuity, which continues to this day. It's all part of the culture now for people to acknowledge that sexual activity is a normal expectation in a dating relationship. The influence of culture should never be underestimated, for it can potentially challenge people to accept ways that are contrary to personally treasured values. Nevertheless, we always have choices and I illustrate with a personal story.

I remember one day after Christmas a few years ago that my wife and I decided to go watch a movie. The theatre was packed. As we sat down, I noticed there were families all around us with young teenagers. Moments into the movie and the sexually graphic scenes began with foul language. My wife and I immediately looked at each other and we were both thinking the same thing. We got up and quietly made our way to the exit. I felt even better when my wife said that she was going to get our money back as the movie was offensively mis-rated, and she did. Then we walked through the mall, drank a bubble tea, and talked about our counter-cultural experience. My point is that we are not necessarily compelled to conform to the suggestions of cultural thought. In that case it was its mis-rating of a movie. Sure, some of our Christian friends, and some of you, don't see it that way. Go ahead and call it Christian legalism (note the discussion on legalism in the 2nd chapter), but you should acknowledge that the convictions of Christ followers can be nonplused by culture force.

Nevertheless, effective discipleship entails growing in discernment and focusing on the grand theme of peoples' need of grace. I remember years ago when I was a young Christian standing in the lobby of the head office of a major bank in downtown Toronto where I worked, and waiting for a streetcar. An impeccably dressed bank executive whom I recognized was also waiting, but he wasn't waiting for a streetcar. I acknowledged him and he nodded back. We made small talk as he was fidgeting. He asked me where I was going, and I told him I was headed to a Bible study. With the zeal of a recent convert, I explained briefly how Jesus had come into my life and changed me. Then he looked at me, and said seriously, "I think there is some room in my life for Jesus too." As he finished speaking, an attractive young lady who was not his wife met him and they dashed off together. Who knows? Maybe I sowed a seed in him. The Gospel is intended to forgive, restore, heal, and fulfill a person, *any* person. If we long to impact the lives of people we must do so one person at a time and developing relationships, while being spiritually fortified by the reality of Christ in us. There are many Christians in all vocations, neighbourhoods, and various circles of influence, who can make a difference.

Without pushiness, we should engage people by not antagonizing them. In His Sermon on the Mount, Jesus said expressly, "Do not give what is holy to the dogs; nor cast your pearls before swine, lest they trample them under their feet, and turn and tear you in pieces" (Matt. 7:6). For various reasons, some may be unprepared to receive what we consider as the pricelessness of God's wonderful grace. The reaction is often exactly as described by Jesus. People can become like "dogs" and "swines" and "trample" our "pearls . . . under their feet." Cultural thought cannot understand how SC can be so appealing, but a Christian mind can identify completely with Paul's exclamations: "Oh, the depth of the riches both of the wisdom and knowledge of God! How unsearchable are His judgements and His ways past finding out!" (Rom. 11:33). We treasure the values of our CF and if we are not savvy exemplars with tempered communications then we can have a negative effect on people. Many confrontations could be avoided by exercising some practical wisdom. Humility, love, kindness, and intelligent engagement with discernment of cultural trends, are what will influence people.

Perhaps the most personally challenging questions I have ever read in Christian literature were written in a letter by one of the most successful disciple makers. I love these questions, and I hope you will appreciate them:

Would those that know nothing of Christ be able to catch and *understand* the true *spirit* and *meaning* of the religion of Jesus by an acquaintance with you? Would they obtain from your *life* and example such an idea of the *nature, design and tendency* of the gospel as would lead them to value it, to understand its necessity and importance?[76]

Aren't these excellent questions? They were asked in 1839, and remain challenging today. Some may think that these questions are not so important in a vastly changed culture where Christian faith is more of an internally kept belief. SC teaches, however: "Now thanks be to God who always leads us in triumph in Christ, and through us diffuses the fragrance of His knowledge in every place" (2 Cor. 2:14). Influential engagement with culture entails understanding what we believe and then living it out with fulfillment. If we are not "affected from above" and not happy in Christ it will show. As was seen, cultural persuasion or dissuasion takes root on the human level. Engaging culture entails knowing how people are being influenced to think and live in society and then interacting with them. I am not strictly alluding to evangelism, though it is integral to discipleship. We impact culture in our societies by demonstrating our Christian discipline, refrain, graciousness, genuine respect for our colleagues and superiors, humility in success, and by our radiant joy.

You will then be surprised how people will respond positively to your invitation to attend a Christian meeting, for when we interact with people our true characters will show. Peoples'

---

[76] Charles G. Finney, "Professor Finney's Letter of February 13, 1839: To The Converts of the Great Revivals That Have Prevailed in the United States Within the Few Last Years" In *The Promise of the Spirit*, Timothy L. Smith, ed. and comp. (Minneapolis: Bethany House Publishers, 1980), 60. Italics are from the text.

characteristics and traits always reveal themselves to those with whom it comes into contact. Impatient people get easily rattled in traffic and cashier line-ups, and it shows. Proud people are unteachable, and cannot handle being wrong in conversation. They like to do all the talking. You know the type. Miserable people are often cantankerous, contentious, and irritable. They also have difficulty smiling. You know where I am going with this. What are the characteristics and traits of us as Christians? How do we demonstrate the power of SC in our lives? What would make anyone desire what we have? I can recite here the beautiful fruits of the Spirit as taught by Paul in Galatians 5, but let's be frank. We have referred to the fruits of the Spirit ad infinitum in our fellowships, books, teachings, seminars, and yet many believers lack almost all of them. Perhaps the reason why cultural icons and pop cultural characters garner many followers is because they demonstrate something that appeals to people and makes others wish to identify.

How can Christians attract followers? It must begin with each one of us. The fruits of the Spirit have been mentioned, but for now let's focus only on these three fruits, "love, joy, kindness," and the others will surely follow (Gal. 5:22-23). When we love people, we will be careful with our words, because as adults we know that contrary to the primary school rhyme names and words can really hurt. Paul knew the importance of our tongues when he wrote: "Let your speech always be with grace, seasoned with salt, that you may know how you ought to answer each one" (Col. 4:6). Of course, we all know what James said about the tongue: "It is an unruly evil, full of deadly poison" (3:8). Our love should demonstrate itself also by words. Joy too must be a wholehearted attribute of our CF. If you are not fulfilled with your CF what makes you think anyone else would desire it? Joy springs from the Spirit within and exudes from your countenance. This morning on Twitter I watched a short video by a Christian I am following. She was receiving medical attention for her disease and her countenance was radiating joy. It was quite moving to see her talk and remain genuinely happy. The Spirit is inside of her and she has grown in its fruit of joy with a powerful witness. Kindness too is a very powerful and attractive spiritual trait. It is the opposite of rudeness. Test your kindness and courteousness the next time you speak with a customer service representative about your bill. If the reps knew you were a Christian what would they think about you and your CF? Only a growing reality of Jesus in our lives can increase these characteristics and make them an irresistibly sweet fragrance.

He is the only way forward. Some time with Jesus every day is vital to a lifestyle of discipleship, and growing in *knowingness*. Learning at the school of Jesus, and then discerning the culture is the most exciting endeavour imaginable. This stuff is wonderfully real. Those of you with whom this is resonating know exactly what I am talking about. As a Christian, you cannot compete with cultural forces without having a depth of understanding in SC. The innuendos, criticism, sarcasm, and arrogant dismissals of the validity of CF by the subtle communications in movies, television programs, and the internet, have been to the chagrin of many believers. Such pounding can take its toll on Christians who are trying to "fight the good fight of faith" (1 Tim. 6:12). Every Christian knows how much of a battle it can be. Accordingly, we need to study and understand for ourselves everything Paul meant when he said,

> Stand therefore, having girded your waist with truth, having put on the breastplate of righteousness, and having shod your feed with the preparation of the gospel of peace; above all, taking the shield of faith with which you will be able to quench all the fiery darts of the wicked one. And take the helmet of salvation, and the sword of the Spirit, which is the word of God, praying always with all prayer and supplication in the Spirit" (Eph. 5: 14-18).

A preacher cannot impart the powers of this passage to you. You must dig deep into it, with careful meditation and study to discover precisely what it all means for *your* CF.

In North America, lifestyle discipleship is now reaching a fork in the road. We will either allow the culture to continue to influence us, and erode our CF, or we will discern what is happening and begin to engage it intelligently. Mainstream culture has successfully influenced churches and entire denominations. I am concerned that it is only a matter of time until cultural thought influences laws to restrict what Christians can and cannot say, which would then send SC underground in North America. Cultural thought is slowly trying to squeeze us out of the realm of legitimate belief and conversation. Do not think that it can't happen. Dickerson also said, "The United States has shifted into a postmodern and post-Christian age. Nobody contests this. The real question is, . . . How long until changing beliefs reshape legislation, institutions, and cultural norms . . . ?"[77] Honestly, I believe secularism is eating our lunch; hopefully, our disciple making initiatives will impact one person at a time before secularism eats our breakfast and dinner too.

There are many examples of how culture is eating our lunch. Insomuch that a lifestyle of discipleship is now discouraged from mentioning such terms as, sin, repentance, holiness, and sexual immorality. As was abundantly shown, the Gospel begins with "repentance." Culture is pressuring ministries to be embarrassed of these biblical terms. In Paul's final exhortation to the Ephesian elders he said with emotion, "For I have not shunned to declare to you *the whole counsel of God*" (Acts 20:27). Our generation is also entrusted with declaring "the whole counsel of God." We too must apply ourselves to helping people make sense of sin and how human endeavour can never overcome its power. Innuendoes from cultural thought that SC is embarrassing to thinking people should not cause us to refrain, but present us with a challenge to roll up our sleeves and communicate SC intelligently. We should exit our comfort zones and apply ourselves to becoming insightful, knowledgeable, and loving disciple makers. Insightfulness means acknowledging what cultural thought is saying in society, for the information conveyed is in the very air we breathe. Then listen intently, learning when to speak, how to speak, and when to express temperate disagreements. Our conversation should reveal that we are not living in a vacuum with our SC.

---

[77] Dickerson, *The Great Evangelical Recession*, 41-42. As a Canadian, I can attest that the citation applies equally to Canada.

If every believer in every field, industry, vocation, or institution reflected the power of SC then more people would find the grace of God and experience His restoration. Cultural thought would also have far less criticism of believers. As one Christian journalist commented astutely in *Popcultured*:

> Our most powerful message is who we are. Imagine if the only Christians that Hollywood writers knew were strong, assured, rational, caring, forgiving, loving, sincere, exciting, lively, wise and joyful people. Then they'd have far less excuse for portraying us in a negative light. In fact, to do so would then bring them into disrepute for failing to be observant. If our own houses were in order, others might listen more attentively.[78]

Thus, we are reminded by Scripture: "He who says he abides in Him ought himself also to walk just as He walked" (1 Jn. 2:6). Believers must grow in the *knowingness* that Jesus is indeed our "chief cornerstone, elect, precious, and he who believes on Him will by no means be put to shame" (1 Pet. 2:6).

We cannot delude ourselves, however, that disciple making is *completely* counter-cultural, because it is not. As I noted, we live in society and participate in similar activities as our non-Christian friends and neighbours. Realistically, Christianity can never separate completely from culture to form a whole new sub-culture. I remember when our son was 7 or 8 years old how our family

---

[78] Steve Turner, *Popcultured: Thinking Christianly About Style, Media and Entertainment* (Downers Grove: InterVarsity Press, 2013), 219-220.

would join both Christian and non-Christian families for day trips, or to watch a movie, and then we would all go out for dinner. We invited both Christian and non-Christian friends and family to celebrate our son's birthdays at various venues. All believers are part of a wider culture outside of their communities of faith, and not everything in culture is contrary to SC. If we were to stick only to ourselves we would be disobedient to the Lord's great commission to "make disciples of all the nations, baptizing them in the name of the Father and of the Son and of the Holy Spirit, *teaching them* to observe all things that I have commanded you" (Matt. 28:19). We cannot "make disciples" and "teach them" unless we engage them, and that entails exercising a lifestyle discipleship within the context of our culture.

We should dispel even the slightest thought that if we truly commit to carrying out this great commission our lives will be lusterless. Intense interest should grip every Christian that has experienced the "beautiful pearl." Such an indelible experience inspires a way of life that moves in awestruck wonder that God is *real*. Knowing His grace personally should be so life impacting that it affects us comprehensively. A believer will discover that the more one studies SC the more intriguing it becomes to the intellect, for the ways of God are truly deep and "unsearchable." "For as the heavens are higher than the earth," says the Lord, "so are My ways higher than your ways, and My thoughts than your thoughts" (Is. 55:9). A lifestyle of discipleship will be intellectually fascinated with how CF grapples with the God whose capacities are unlike ours. Consider this Psalm of David (reminder from Chapter 2 to read Scripture intently and meditatively):

O LORD, You have searched me and known me. You know my sitting down and my rising up; You understand my thoughts afar off. You comprehend my path and my lying down, and are acquainted with all my ways. For there is not a word on my tongue, but behold, O LORD, You know it altogether. You have hedged me behind and before, and laid your hand upon me. Such knowledge is too wonderful for me; it is high, I cannot attain it (139:1-6).

What a direct human experience with the Almighty! If you have the "witness of the Spirit" in you then reading that passage should strike you with unending marvel at how "such knowledge is too wonderful." David continued, "For you formed my inward parts; You covered me in my mother's womb. I will praise You, for I am fearfully and wonderfully made; marvelous are your works, *and that my soul knows very well*" (Ps. 139: 13-14). Our inner most being can know His marvelous works "very well."

Let us exercise some reason here. The human mind is capable of accomplishing the near impossible. It landed men on the moon. It has engineered mighty machines and fascinating structures. Almost instantly, it can track countless of financial transactions globally. It can analyze matter and display its research by breathtaking images. If David was correct that we are "fearfully and wonderfully made" then what about our Maker? What can He do? Then Paul was correct that, "the riches both of the wisdom and knowledge of God" are deep. Isaiah was also correct when he revealed that God's "ways" are higher than our "ways" and God's "thoughts" are higher than our "thoughts." Our rapidly secularizing culture, however, does not like this line of reasoning. With its aura of sophistication and a self-absorbed assumption of its scientific prowess, cultural thought relishes in being the gadfly to believers.

Take for instance the question often adduced, who made God? It's illogical and yet it continues with gusto even by people who should know better. First, the question can only be asked meaningfully if God does exist. If He doesn't, the question is a non sequitur, that is, nothing follows that warrants a discussion because there is nothing to talk about. With no existence, no answer can make sense. The question alludes to the classic Watchmaker's argument of William Paley (1743-1805) wherein an intricate watch has a watchmaker, and so it follows that the intricacies of the universe must likewise have a Designer. The skeptic concedes that the watch had a watchmaker, but not that the universe had a Designer/God. Thus, the question persists, who made God? The question on who created the watch does follow, because there is a watchmaker we can discuss. If the question on who made the Designer/God is to be meaningful the questioner must also accept God's existence and be open to the answer wherever it leads. Open-mindedness to God's attributes will reveal a Being who created things that are different from Himself. He created time, space, matter, and possesses attributes that are beyond the observable. At the very, very least, the questioner should concede to Deism as did the lifelong skeptic and atheist, Antony Flew (1923-2010). Flew became reasonable and changed his position from atheism to Deism by the compelling evidence of design in the universe, and wrote a book on how his thinking process changed.[79]

The presumptions of culture now challenge a Christian's happiness in the reasonableness of CF. Resisting belief in God, and particularly in CF, are increasingly revealing the default position of cultural thought, which is, Scriptural indifference. Anytime a conversation gets compelling the common words which have now become the final arbiter in culture are "I disagree." Regardless of the cogency or meticulous reasoning of some distinguished Christian thinkers cultural thought remains unflinching in its skepticism. Secularism is doing quite a number on people, but we should nevertheless continue to exemplify a lifestyle of discipleship with love and patience towards everyone.

When distinguished apologists stand before hostile audiences that are steeped in secular humanism what makes them defend CF is not their intellectual giftedness. Neither does their depth of knowledge of various disciplines prepare them to confront the skepticism in such an intimidating environment. Surely intellectual giftedness and knowledge are essentials for the task, but what drives apologists is their profound personal experience of CF. *Knowingness* is alive and unmistakable in them, from which they can receive divine strength to engage effectively with the unbelief of secular humanism. When gifted intellectual Christians articulate a case for CF their display of knowledge is always impressive and respectable, but it is their deep experience of grace which they

---

[79] Antony Flew, *There is a God: How the World's Most Notorious Atheist Changed His Mind* (New York: Harper Collins, 2007).

desire for everyone else that impassions them to defend against atheistic thought.

On any level, discipleship must grow in personal knowingness of Jesus in order to overcome the unrelenting impugnments of the culture's indifference towards SC. Nowadays a passive lifestyle of discipleship is easier and any voids can be filled with the latest entertainments. The popularity of many television programs, for example, provides an entertainment value for both Christian and non-Christian viewers. The problem is that without a profound sense of Christ in our lives we become passive and are often entertained blindly, whereas we should be active with our discipleship and offer meaningful critique and ministry. As one Christian thinker keenly called to attention,

> Humans sit in front of television sets, passively watching human misery unfold, while just outside their door, down the street, or in an apartment next door, a real person faces the same problem and there is no one to help them because we're all preoccupied with our favourite characters or reality TV. When diversion becomes a way of life, we avoid the very issues to which we should be more attentive. We are diverted from the grim, unpleasant truth that our lives lack meaning without God, that consumption does not satisfy, that the differential between wealth and poverty is unjust, that out neighbour is in

need, and that appropriate human response to people in need is sleeves-rolled up service, not simply watching.[80] Indeed, Jesus said, "The harvest truly is great, but the labourers are few . . . " (Lk. 10:2). If "the labourers" do not find their work fulfilling then "the harvest" will be neglected.

We should know that our culture will never ingratiate itself with the Scriptural teaching of CF. The general understanding of the Bible is that it is poetic literature at best, and completely fictional at worse. Can you imagine how contemporary people would react to Jesus's words: "unless you repent you will all likewise perish" (Lk. 13:5). They would probably feel offended, but this is the Gospel. We must concentrate on somehow making such language relatable to contemporary people, rather than altogether abandoning its import. Otherwise many believers will continue to be influenced by the biblical illiteracy of our times and become increasingly distant from the power of SC. If Christians fail to discern cultural thinking, and within themselves begin to negotiate SC, they will bereft themselves of the "abundant life." On Sundays, they will worship Jesus and affirm SC but during the week it will be cultural thought that continues to shape many of them.

Even though we have "the light of the world," contemporary culture can be likened to a dimmer switch. Believers realize that in many ways they continue to identify with how their non-Christian friends and neighbours are living. There is much participation in

---

[80] Dick Staub, *The Culturally Savvy Christian: A Manifesto For Deepening Faith And Enriching Popular Culture In An Age of Christianity-Lite* (San Francisco: John Wiley & Sons, Inc. 2007), 7.

the same activities, talking about the same television programs, discussing the latest news, communicating on social media, and play dates for their kids are arranged while tea and conversation about things in culture are enjoyed. Now again, such is part of a normal lifestyle of discipleship in polite society and I encourage relationships. When good and healthy ones are established with our non-Christian neighbours and friends they can be influenced by our interaction. Sometimes even a simple offer of prayer can go a long way. When love and grace are effectively communicated even an explanation of Luke 13:5 can influence an attentive listener. The dilution of SC, however, in order to befriend cultural thought is a snare. CF remains compelling and people are searching for inner fulfillment. How we model and communicate SC can influence the lives of others beyond our expectations.

A lifestyle of discipleship is from the inside out and not the outside in. Paul said, "I have been crucified with Christ; it is no longer I who live, but Christ lives in me . . . " (Gal. 2:20). Such Christian language would shock anyone outside of that personal experience. What? Give up my life and allow Christ to take over? Where is the fun in that? A secular thinking person in today's culture finds such a proposition of CF, to put it mildly, repulsive. Moreover, the repulsiveness is manifested in culture by various subtleties. Sure, most people are polite about their aversions to CF. Nevertheless, believers experience the rejection of culture as a perturbing challenge to what they hold dearly *within*. Thus "spiritual warfare" is real as forces are constantly challenging a lifestyle of discipleship to keep its personal experience of Christ within oneself, but it's not meant to be contained. As Paul also said, "to live is Christ" (Philip. 1:21).

What I am pointing out is that it becomes quite a challenge for us to express our CF outside of our church walls when we are pretty much like everyone else in culture. Our light shines bright at church but it is dimmed by the overwhelming influences of what cultural thought is conveying. A lifestyle of discipleship will surely require of us to engage with people and to love them, but the existential challenges to nurturing "the seed" that landed "on the good ground" of our lives (Matt. 13:23) are definitely taking their toll on North American faith communities.

People in culture are becoming indifferent to our beliefs, and yet they continue to share meaningfully in our relationships with them. Our calling to become effective disciple makers could easily lose its identity, as we are affected by secularism and blending in society accordingly. We must nurture our inner experience of grace, grow to enjoy it, and learn how to become effective exemplars of CF towards others. For us, the most effective practice now is to take note of what James taught, "let every man be swift to hear, slow to speak, slow to wrath" (1:19). Doing more listening than speaking is an important lesson we ought to learn from SC. When people are listened to, they become more open, and they also appreciate their listeners more. Opportunities to make love contributions, kindness contributions, and empathy contributions, in the lives of people will increase our credibility as disciples. As Paul also encouraged, "And let us not grow weary while doing good, for in due season we shall reap if we do not lose heart" (Gal. 6:9).

Most assuredly, the more we adhere to what James taught in that passage the more we ourselves will grow wiser by understanding how desperately people are in need of the Lord's restoration. In a recent article, "Non-Christians want to talk faith, but don't see Christians as good listeners," it was noted by

> Brooke Hempell, senior vice-president of research at the Barna Group . . . that the findings showed that 'as we find popular culture increasingly distanced from Christianity, non-Christians may need a lot more time to digest and come to terms with what the Gospel proposes or offers them. . . . We have to go slow! Take the time to build familiarity and appreciation of the non-believer's context first, then build trust, then discuss - not just lecture.'[81]

Empathy towards peoples' life situations and hearing them out will be paramount for a lifestyle of discipleship that is committed to making the grace of God known. These traits are now indispensable to maintaining a consistent Christian witness in North American culture. People cannot see, feel, or touch our inner experience of CF, but they can observe our interactions with them by our ears, mouths, and actions. Our words and manners are what others can experience. Good listening is not only a requirement of SC, but it is also indicative of genuine care and concern for someone's personal challenges. CF can only be perceived as credible by how its representatives affect others in conversation and relationships. Love, kindness, courteousness,

---

[81] Michael Gryboski, "Non-Christians want to talk faith, but don't see Christians as good listeners, Barna finds," *Christian Post* (February 25, 2019): Online, *https://www.christianpost.com/news/non-christians-want-to-talk-faith-but-dont-see-christians-as-good-listeners-barna-finds.html*.

"swift to hear, slow to speak," remain indispensable and non-negotiable Christian practices.

Finally, the experience of God's grace in the Lord Jesus is *real*, and you have the "pearl of great price." I pray that you will continue to explore all He has for you, and that you will increasingly realize that SC continues to compel and reveal itself to provide incomparable fulfillment to hungry hearts and open minds. Your lifestyle of discipleship is in possession of what everyone around you is looking for. The world is broken and your place in it with the grace of God residing in you can make a wonderful difference. Should we cross paths be sure to introduce yourself. So that we may ask one another, What have you been learning from the Lord Jesus lately?

About the Author

Marlon De Blasio was born and raised in downtown Toronto, where he continues to reside. He was not raised in a Christian home, but found Christ at the age of twenty-three. He has been happily married to Felicia for over twenty-two years, and they have a son, Nathan. Marlon has travelled extensively. He is a notable Christian thinker, guest speaker, teacher, and lecturer, with a keen interest in Christian Discipleship, Cultural theology and apologetics. It has been said that Marlon has "a passion for Christian faith, and all it entails, that is rare."

As time permits, Felicia and Marlon enjoy serving and volunteering. They also enjoy hosting and the company of people from various backgrounds, nationalities, and cultures. Marlon is an avid reader, book collector, conversationalist, and enjoys long walks in downtown Toronto.

He graduated from Tyndale University College with a B. Th. and earned several academic awards. He then enrolled at Trinity Evangelical Divinity School, Trinity International University, and graduated with an M. A., Cum Laude, and was awarded Thesis of the Year in the ST dept. At Trinity, he was also elected to Who's Who Among Students in American Universities and Colleges. Marlon earned his Ph. D. in Theology/Philosophy at St. Michael's College, University of Toronto.

You can follow him on Twitter@MarlonDeBlasio.